W9-BNU-495

Making the
Big Move

*How to transform relocation into
a creative life transition*

CATHY GOODWIN, PH.D.

New Harbinger Publications, Inc.

Publisher's Note

This publication is designed to provide accurate and authoritative information in regard to the subject matter covered. It is sold with the understanding that the publisher is not engaged in rendering psychological, financial, legal, or other professional services. If expert assistance or counseling is needed, the services of a competent professional should be sought.

Distributed in the U.S.A. by Publishers Group West; in Canada by Raincoast Books; in Great Britain by Airlift Book Company, Ltd.; in South Africa by Real Books, Ltd.; in Australia by Boobook; and in New Zealand by Tandem Press.

New Harbinger Publications, Inc.
5674 Shattuck Avenue
Oakland, CA 94609

Cover design by Blue Design (www.bluedes.com)
Cover illustration by Anne Smith
Edited by Andrew Liotta
Text design by Tracy Marie Powell

Library of Congress Catalog Card Number: 98-68751
ISBN 1-57224-135-7 Paperback

New Harbinger Publications' Website address: www.newharbinger.com

01   00   99

10   9   8   7   6   5   4   3   2   1

First printing

Contents

PART 3   Special Situations

Acknowledgments

Thanks to all those who generously shared their stories. A special thanks to those who devoted extra time to telephone, e-mail, and personal interviews, especially Linda Hoge, Rita McMillian, Rob Warren, Stacey Baker, Gerrard Macintosh, and JoAnn Wolfram. Sharon and Richard Parker shared many stories and provided long-distance encouragement throughout the project. Joan Lerner and Michael Mayo contributed helpful insights from their experience as therapists. Carole Macklin of the Society for Consumer Psychology invited me to organize our 1997 conference, which brought me to the New Harbinger exhibit booth. I enjoyed generous reference support from the Free Library of Philadelphia and the Einstein Library at Nova Southeastern University in Fort Lauderdale. The New Harbinger editors—Angela Watrous, Farrin Jacobs, Kristin Beck, and Andrew Liotta—were incredibly patient, constructive, and helpful throughout the process.

I must also thank the various organizations and individuals who wreaked havoc on my own moves over the years, thereby teaching me valuable lessons and providing magificent examples for this book.

Introduction

So you're thinking about moving. Maybe you're starting a new job. Or maybe you're moving to keep the one you already have. You might just want to live closer to your children or maybe it's time to retire. Are you having a hard time deciding? Perhaps the decision has been made for you.

Like most people who move, you are faced with a major life transition. But that's not all. You may also be facing a logistical nightmare. There are schedules to keep. Time constraints mean pressure. Jobs and moving vans follow timetables that do not leave room for a crisis. Yet nearly every relocation story includes a crisis, large or small: a child comes down with the measles, the car breaks down, the cat stops eating. Each crisis demands attention and depletes energy. Even with careful planning, one unexpected crisis can destroy a lot of hard work. How are you going to navigate this minefield when your compass has been taken away?

I wrote *Making the Big Move* after conducting interviews with people who had been through relocations. As a college professor who has enjoyed a lifetime of relocation, I was naturally drawn to research about life transitions. At the close of each interview, people would ask me, Why don't we have some guidance? There's nobody out there who understands what I'm going through. Why do things always seem to go wrong at the last minute? How can you select a location where you will fit in easily? How can you ease the transition to a new home? And what can you do if you realize you've made a mistake?

You can find plenty of advice on the practical aspects of moving, such as how to pack or how to buy a house, but the deeper questions go unanswered. How do you stay in touch with who you are while your physical world is shifting around you? How do you not only survive, but grow? What do you do when your new home seems to violate every aspect of your identity?

In order to answer these questions, you must ask yourself the bigger questions: Who am I? Can I still be me after I move? And what if I don't like the person I'm becoming?

Major life transitions force you to revise the way you view yourself and the world around you. The results of such transitions are as varied as the people who go through them. For some, moving can be a source of grief and stress, as it is a form of loss, an end of security, an upheaval. For others, however, moving can be a source of growth. It can even be fun. Each new city holds new opportunities for discovery and adventure.

The book's premise is simple. Your home offers a way for you to express your identity. Your activities and possessions, as well as your interactions with neighbors and colleagues, proclaim, "This is who I am." When you move, you have to find new ways to express yourself and to deal with those who do not view you the same way. By dealing with these challenges, you find yourself negotiating with yourself and with others to arrive at a new identity. This identity negotiation may be stressful, but by accepting the challenge you can not only survive but transform and grow; you can make moving a creative transition.

How to Use This Book

This book has been designed as a practical guide that you can use from the moment you consider moving to the moment you hear yourself saying, "This is home." To gain maximum benefit, skim the whole book first to gain an overview.

The goal is to help you take advantage of your moving as an opportunity for personal growth. By getting acquainted with the information and working through the exercises you will be able to discover more about who you are and perhaps find some clues about who you want to be. Creativity is part discovery and part invention, and it is my hope that this book will help you to do both, while making your transition a smooth and rewarding experience.

The book is divided into three parts. Part 1, Choosing to Make the Move, focuses on the steps you need to take to make the big decision. Sorting through the details of moving and uncovering sources of stress will help you face your fears and understand what moving means to you. You will learn that who you are is intricately connected to where you live and that understanding your identity can help you assess how well you will fit into your future destination. If the gaps are too wide, you may decide not to move at all. If you have no choice, you can plan ways to survive an undesirable move. The information you find and the lessons you learn about yourself in part 1 will help you with the decision to move. Will the new place be right for you? Can you be happy there? If not, can you create a survival plan to keep going until you can move again?

Part 2, Making the Big Move, takes you through the transition step by step. I have broken down the process into five phases. In the *Separation Phase* you acknowledge the life you've lived in your current residence and say good-bye to the things you can't take with you. During this phase you can use the comfort of a familiar location to help you find a new home and prepare for the turmoil to come. In the *Transformation Phase* you leave your old home and arrive in your new location. In this in-between period you no longer belong in your old life and have yet to find your new one. In your new home, you'll begin the *Integration Phase (The First Six Months)*. This is often a time for grieving, but it can also be a time for self-discovery and increased creativity. In the *Integration Phase (After Six Months)* you'll find yourself slowly settling in to your new roles. In general, this period lasts until about the two year mark. Finally, in the *Maintenance Phase,* you'll work to maintain your new life in your new location as you either settle in comfortably or start facing your next move. Throughout these chapters you will find exercises and information that will help you see yourself clearly as you navigate each step in the process and slowly redefine yourself, adapting your identity to your new location. You'll be surprised that along with the stress comes increased opportunities for self-expression and discovery.

In part 3, Special Situations, you will find information and exercises that focus on specific problems some movers face: dealing with resistance, moving with a family, moving on your own, moving out of the country, moving with a corporate sponsor, and finally using the skills you've learned to help a loved one through their relocation.

By working through this book you will come out with a new perspective on relocation that can enable you to prepare for the road ahead, smoothing bumps before you get to them.

You may want to invest in a journal or open a new file on your computer where you can complete the exercises. Having all of your answers and insights in one place will help you focus on the issues of your transformation, and since some of the exercises refer to other exercises, having them all in one place will be helpful. You may also want to look back at your observations when you've settled in, or when you plan a second move.

Stress Wastes Time

Your first reaction may be, "This is a lot of work. And I have to move!" If you're trying to juggle a move while winding down a job or preparing the children, you may feel that you already have your hands full. You're under enough stress as it is without trying to find time for self-discovery.

What you might not realize is that all that stress might be wasting a lot of time. Stress can distort your perceptions. A fearful, anxious person will make poor decisions, leading to more problems. Stress saps your energy. Time spent worrying is time spent depleting energy that you are desperately going to need during a turbulent transition.

As you work through the exercises in this book, you'll reduce stress in a number of ways. You'll feel a sense of control as you plan. You'll become more aware of your needs, values, and feelings. As a result, you will gain increased energy and efficiency as you make decisions during this transition. The time you invest in exploring your identity will come back to you with interest. You will probably feel that you have gained several hours in your day, and you will undoubtedly be using them more happily and productively. The more relaxed you are, the more smoothly your move will go. When you work through your stress and face your fears, you may find that problems seem to solve themselves.

Three Moves in Eight Years

I have lived this book. For most of my adult life, I have moved every two years, sometimes more often. Even when I remained in one city, I often moved from one apartment to another. I've enjoyed corporate-paid moves with a national moving company and I've struggled to fit all my possessions into a compact car. Twice I've used airfreight and once I sent luggage ahead by Greyhound. I've lived all over North America, from Alaska to Atlanta.

I began writing this book in Philadelphia—a city I love. I had the perfect apartment, with everything I wanted in easy walking distance. An unusual opportunity brought me to South Florida, a part of the country I had seen only in movies and TV cop shows, and yes, everything went wrong—well, almost everything. I had limited time to search for a place to live. My "rental wanted" ad was delayed by an e-mail glitch and displayed with an incorrect telephone number. I fell in love with an apartment, only to learn that it would take a month to approve me as a tenant. I ended up moving to a place that seemed nothing like the Real Me. The car I was going to buy became unavailable at the last minute. The moving company—a household name—sent their worst packing team to load my shipment. They broke glass tables, lost my new prints, and scuffed almost everything else. I drove twelve hundred miles in a crowded rental car with two cats who weren't speaking to me by the time we reached our destination. I had to draw on all the advice contained in this book.

Moving is like climbing a mountain. You become more skillful with each climb, and it helps if you have access to the best equipment on the market. Good weather and good luck don't hurt. Once you've climbed one mountain, you have to start all over again if you want to climb another. Even if you're experienced, you'll still have to deal with sore muscles and ice storms. Each peak offers its own challenges, but also its own unique opportunity for excitement, adventure, challenge, and growth. Memories of pain fade as you reach the heights and survey your conquest. Some day you may be ready to try again, or you may decide you've had enough adventure for a lifetime. It is my hope that this book will help as you make your way to the top of your next peak.

PART 1

Choosing to Make the Move

1

"Why Do I Dread This Move?"

What Moving Means to You

This should be an exciting time. You're thinking about moving. You're standing on the threshold of a new life, poised for adventure. The future holds all sorts of exciting possibilities. So why do you feel that sense of dread in the pit of your stomach?

Moving is complicated, both physically and emotionally. Your desk holds a dozen "to do" lists filled with unfamiliar tasks. One small problem can explode into a large-scale disaster. Your feelings are equally unfamiliar. You feel sad as you bid good-bye to your friends, your neighbors, even your garden. You feel scared as you wonder if you'll ever find another house as comfortable as the one you're in now. At the same time, you're eager to take on a new job and curious about what you'll be doing next year.

When you're feeling overwhelmed, you may find yourself wondering, "Why did I ever think about moving in the first place?" When this happens you need to take a step back to get a look at the big picture. You might not be able to solve all the problems immediately, but at least you can identify them, and that's the first step toward a solution. So try to sort this tangle of emotions into more manageable threads. Maybe then you can figure out why you're feeling so much stress and gain a sense of control.

More Than a Change of Address

Moving involves taking you and your possessions from one location to another. Yet the physical aspects of the move are only a small part of the experience. Your possessions probably look the same after they're taken off the moving van as they did when they were loaded on. Yet something is definitely different. Perhaps the biggest change is in the way you view yourself and the world around you. Familiar beliefs and behaviors may now seem out of place. Tasks that you once completed smoothly and effortlessly may now seem clumsy and slow. You may start to examine yourself and realize you're looking at a whole new person—a person you barely recognize.

Significant life transitions force people to reconsider their identities. Most people recognize that marriage, divorce, graduation, and childbirth are significant life transitions. Ceremonies and rituals, such as weddings, funerals, and graduations, mark many of these life transitions and often provide you with evidence of your new identity: "After the wedding, I'll be known as the husband;" "After graduation, I get to put some initials after my name."

Moving is an equally significant life transition, but no formal ceremonies exist to mark your passage. Getting a new driver's license, changing your address, and ordering utilities are viewed as chores. They do not transform you into a "resident." Nor do they announce your new status to others. After all you've been through, you're still a newcomer, and, often, an outsider, for a long time afterward.

Some Moving Facts

In 1990, the United States Census Bureau estimated that 17 percent of the population moves each year—that's more than forty million people. About seven million of those people move from one state to another. Despite these numbers, surprisingly little help is available to those who move. Moving companies and websites offer basic information about the logistics of moving. Most books focus on the practical side of moving: how to pack, how to look for a house, how to choose a real estate agent. These books rarely mention the emotional issues involved in moving.

Nearly everyone experiences some form of emotional pain when they relocate. Debbie, an administrative assistant who moved to Texas from Chicago, confided that she sought medical advice for anxiety attacks. "I didn't know what was wrong," she said. "I thought I was crazy." Latisha, a dental hygienist, recalled moving her family to Boston so her husband could attend law school. "The kids cried for six months," she said. Marvin, a college professor, felt lucky to get a tenure-track position in a tiny college town in the Great Plains area. But after the first year, he was worried he would have to move. "My wife can't get a job here. We need her income; but more importantly she needs a career to stay sane."

When people seek help, they often find little understanding from friends and family. Even professional health providers can feel baffled when confronted with clients who say, "I just moved and I'm miserable!"

Relatively few studies have been conducted on the topic of voluntary relocation. The academic and popular presses publish many more articles on the psychology of divorce, bereavement, and midlife crisis. The result is that most people don't understand the emotional upheaval connected with moving.

A Brief History of Moving

Relocation represents a recent cultural and historical phenomenon. Only within the last fifty years have people experienced mobility at the level of the nuclear family, let alone as individuals. For centuries people have crossed national borders to escape oppression or migrated in search of economic opportunities not available at home. But they usually moved in large groups with their extended families. Young people sometimes moved in order to find work—schoolteachers, apprentices, and servants frequently left home at young ages—but their experiences were considerably different from those of young people today. They were assigned to board with families and therefore they faced stifling confinement as opposed to the isolation and wide range of choices that many people find today.

In the modern world, mobility requires affluence and education. Moving costs money and few people benefit economically from a move unless their skills are in demand. Warren, a social worker in Seattle, said, "People come to Seattle because they hear they can get work at one of the big companies here. The reality is that these companies recruit from all over the country. If they need your skills, they will find you and pay your way to Seattle. I see so many disappointed people every year."

The notion of corporate transfers is a relatively new one. In his book *JobShift*, William Bridges (1994) notes that the notion of a job with seniority, transfers, and benefits has evolved since World War II. If you're a baby boomer, your parents belonged to the first generation to view such relocations as common place. Before the 1970s, these relocations usually meant that everyone moved when the husband was transferred. The full-time wife and mother handled all the chores and developed the family's social life. Single people rarely moved for professional reasons and rarely bought their own homes.

When a social pattern emerges quickly, a society does not have time to develop practices and structures to cope effectively. You cannot draw strength from traditions or legends. You may not know how to obtain or offer help. When it comes to moving, many people empathize with the woman I interviewed who said, "Frankly, I don't even know what I'm supposed to be feeling right now."

Your own experiences of relocation will most likely color how you feel about moving. What is a move? What images of moving do you bring forward as you plan your own relocation? Before reading further, work through the following exercise.

= Exercise
My Life as a Mover

Get a notebook or open a new file on the word processor. You are about to write your own personal history of moving by answering the following questions:

- How often did you move as a child?

- What were some of the reasons for moving? Do you think you were told the real reasons?

- Were you involved in any aspect of the decision-making process?

- How was the work of the move divided? (This includes packing, selling the old house, finding a new place to live, changing addresses, helping the children, driving or arranging transportation, dealing with movers, cleaning, and any other activities you can recall.) Make a list of what each family member did during the move. What were the roles of your parents, brothers and sisters, grandparents, and other relatives.

- As you recall the moves your family made, what emotions do you remember? Hope? Frustration? Excitement?

- Were there other relocations in your family? (Did your grandparents immigrate to escape war or famine? Did a distant relative move to take a teaching job or become an apprentice?)

- Are there family legends about moving? (Did ancestors move West in covered wagons or immigrate through Ellis Island?) Have you lost touch with relatives because you or they moved?

- Did you hear negative stories about family or friends who moved? For example,

  Uncle Harry will never settle down.

  We never saw Cousin Beatrice after they moved out west.

- Do you recall stories of classmates, friends, or neighbors who moved? How did these stories affect your beliefs about moving? For example,

  I remember when Dennis moved here to Nashville from Tucson, Arizona. He had so many great stories. We all envied him. It seemed so exotic to live in different places.

  My best friend moved away when we were high school sophomores. We wrote back and forth for a while but I never found another best friend. We didn't have e-mail back then and long distance calls were a big deal.

- As you plan to move, how do your past experiences with moving affect you? Do you feel as if your attitude is unrelated to the past or do you feel you're carrying on a tradition? For example,

  As I pack up to move, I hear my mother saying, "A rolling stone gathers no moss." My parents lived in the same house for forty years. I've never spent more than five years in one place.

  My father always went ahead while my mom stayed behind to pack and deal with the movers. She did the social stuff, too. I have to admit I almost envy him, but my wife works full-time, too. We divided the chores but it still feels strange.

Working through this exercise will help you gain perspective on your feelings concerning your move. You may find memories surfacing gradually over a period of weeks and months. You may want to return to this exercise at several stages during your move. Often people are surprised to realize that they come from a family of wanderers. Others realize they are going against everything they learned, often unconsciously, about how people should live.

How Moving Affects Identity

People who move have more physical and financial help than ever. Moving companies compete on price and service. Corporate benefits and tax deductions can ease the financial strain. Yet the first thought of moving creates intense fear and anxiety among most people. In one of the few studies available, Munton (1990) surveyed relocated executives in Britain. Even though these families enjoyed the perks of corporate relocation and the knowledge that a job would be waiting, three-quarters of Munton's respondents reported stress. You may have heard the saying, sometimes attributed to Ben Franklin, "Three moves equal one fire." You may be tempted to respond, "It's the other way around! One move equals three fires."

═══ Exercise ═══
Who Am I?

Before reading further, try this experiment. Writing as fast as you can, find ten answers to the question "Who am I?" in the space below:

1. I am _____

2. I am _____

3. I am _____

4. I am _____

5. I am _____

6. I am _____

7. I am _____

8. I am _____

9. I am _____

10. I am _____

Review what you've written. Each of these statements represents a part of your identity.

What will change if you decide to move?

Moving qualifies as a stressful life event because moving transforms your identity. Did you write, "I am an adopted Californian," or "I'm New England born and bred?" Many people identify strongly with the place where they live. Others take their location for granted. If you didn't identify yourself as a resident or citizen of a place, think how you feel when you return home from a trip, or how you feel when someone asks, "Where are you from?" You may have stronger ties than you realize.

Did you identify yourself as a friend, club member, organization leader? Those roles will change if you move. Even the roles you retain will seem different. If you wrote, "I am a husband," consider how your role will change if you move. You may become the family member who does the laundry or grocery shopping, or you may be faced with a long commute that leaves less time with the family.

Changing Definitions

John and Myrna learned a new meaning of "neighbor" when they moved with their two children to a small Midwestern city. Their children played with the other neighborhood children all winter, but in spring, their neighbors spent weekends at their cottages on the lake. These trips were family-only and outsiders were not invited. John and Myrna were surprised. Where they came from, the neighbor's children were often included in "family" picnics and camping trips. Now, as newcomers, John and Myrna had to explain these new local family values to the children, who felt left out and hurt.

If you move, you may find a different local culture, with different expectations for women, people over fifty, ethnic groups, or people with disabilities. Can a single woman have dinner alone in a restaurant without attracting stares? Will the local merchants be kind and helpful with a child who uses a wheelchair? Do grandmothers wear shorts and T-shirts when the weather gets hot? These customs may seem trivial, but they influence the way you relate to others on a daily basis.

Jeannine, a Seattle native, laughs when she looks back on her three years in the Atlanta area. "I started going out with Brad. After we got serious, we had to have dinner with his parents every Friday night. That was hard to get used to!" She broke up with Brad when she moved back to the West Coast. "Out here," she says now, "everybody is so transient. I hadn't seen my folks for years. I didn't realize that Southern families were still so close. They kept asking me about my family and wondered how I could live so far away."

These lifestyle differences can also affect life on the job. Jeannine was uncomfortable when co-workers spoke about their weekends. Most visited families who lived in the area. Jeannine had no relatives within a thousand miles of her new home. "It seems silly," she says now, "but I felt like an outcast when we talked about our weekends. I realized how different we were."

Interrupting Familiar Routines

Several years ago, a telephone company ran a series of advertisements showing a family that was obviously moving into a new home. The furniture had not arrived and the house was completely empty except for a telephone, sitting in bare splendor on the uncarpeted floor. A woman was happily talking to someone she knew. Now that she had a phone, the woman was saying, she was home. Most people who relocate can relate to the emotions expressed by this ad. When you first move, you feel disconnected. Your first impulse is to reconnect to something familiar and the telephone offers a fast, easy way to do this.

The world is constantly changing. The world you experience today differs considerably from the world you experienced five, ten, or twenty years ago. This kind of change normally occurs very slowly. Computers, VCRs, and microwave ovens entered our lives gradually over a period of years. The way you prepare dinner has slowly evolved from lighting a gas stove to setting a timer for an electric oven to programming the microwave oven. These slow changes could be taken in stride.

But when you move, change happens fast. Imagine that you went to sleep one night in a home containing a manual typewriter, a black-and-white TV, and a gas stove. The next morning you awakened to find those items replaced with a computer, a wide-screen color TV with cable access to hundreds of channels, and an electric stove with a built-in microwave. You would be completely lost! You might be grateful for these appliances after you learned how to use them, but at first you would be confused, frustrated, and completely stressed.

You're accustomed to the way your living room looks. You've probably added furniture one piece at a time, over a period of years. When you move, you are suddenly faced with a bare room as the movers carry out your furniture. Your new home feels different. The city feels different. Sometimes your whole life feels different.

Your identity undergoes a rapid transformation. Over the years, you've become known as "Fran, the best PTA treasurer we ever had," or "Fred who always shows up at the gym on Thursday afternoon." Suddenly, you have a new identity: "Fran the new PTA member" or "Fred who we've never seen at the gym before." Even when your new neighbors extend a warm welcome, you may feel uncomfortable.

Last week, you were on the welcoming committee for your neighborhood and now you're on the receiving end.

The things you take for granted can sometimes cause the greatest confusion in your new relocation. "It's the traffic lights!" said Greg. "This is the only city in the world where we have a green arrow with a red light, meaning it's okay to go straight. I keep seeing the red light and hitting the brake. I've almost been hit three times."

Most people do not realize how many daily routines they perform, or how deeply they are attached to them. An unnoticed routine can become a hot button when they are changed unexpectedly.

== Exercise
Daily Routines

To begin understanding some of your own routines for daily life, start with these three:

Example:

Routine 1: What do I do before going to work on a weekday morning? For example,

> *Wake up without alarm clock → Walk the dog → Dress for work → Drive to the fast food restaurant → Receive greetings from staff (I'm a regular) → Eat breakfast sandwich in my car → Find parking space at the office building.*

Routine 2: What do I do to relax after work in the evening?

Routine 3: How do I spend a Saturday morning?

As you write out your routines, use arrows or diagrams to show progress from one activity to the next. Be as detailed as you like.

After you have completed two or three, put them aside for a day. Return and add details you may have omitted.

Now ask yourself how you would feel about interruptions to these routines. These examples may seem trivial, but it's the trivial changes that often create the greatest difficulty because they go unnoticed.

Moving Means Loss

When your life is interrupted, you must deal with a number of losses, large and small, central or peripheral to your definition of who you are. A loss can be anything you left behind, tangible or intangible. No item is too small to matter. People can mourn a broken fingernail. To answer the question, "How much stress will be produced by the loss?" you need to ask, "How much do I value what I am losing?" People respond very differently to the loss of a pet, a favorite possession, or, as one woman insisted, "the best apartment in the entire city."

Psychologist Stevan Hobfoll (1989) suggests that people have access to resources: money, friends, family, social status, possessions, and skills, and the balance in each person's resource bank can fluctuate. You might lose some money but gain friends or improve skills. A net loss of resources, Hobfoll's theory predicts, will lead to stress.

Moving depletes resources. Even if you gain a pay increase after you move, you have probably given up all sorts of resources that most people take for granted: a social network, the confidence that comes from familiarity, perhaps some favorite activities and possessions. These resources are not easy to replace. For at least some period of time, your resource balance will be lowered.

Although you may not be aware of this loss directly, you may find yourself spontaneously seeking resources. In her book, *The Courage to Grieve*, Judy Tatelbaum (1980) writes that grief creates a sense of "impoverishment." People, therefore, find themselves feeling "needy," wanting a shoulder to cry on, a hug, or just someone to listen.

Feeling needy can be uncomfortable, and a move adds further stress because, being a newcomer, you rarely know where and how to meet even your most mundane needs. If you need a power tool and you don't know where to rent it, you may be reluctant to approach your new neighbors to borrow one. Emotional needs are even more difficult to fulfill. Even if you're lucky enough to find someone who wants to help, they will probably not know what to say when you cry, "I think I've made a mistake! Nothing is working out!"

Dealing with Other Identity Transformations

Moving would be painful enough even if everything else in your life remained stable: your job, your family, and your physical condition. But people rarely move just because they want a change of location. Usually another identity shift occurs simultaneously. You may be moving to get married, to take a new job, or to retire. Each of these transitions brings its own identity interruptions, and losses. When you add relocation to the equation the resulting accumulation of stress can feel explosive.

"I don't know why I'm so upset," said Julie. "Is it my job, which pays less than my old one? Is it the climate, which is giving me allergies? It is living closer to my father, who needs our help more and more? Or is this just part of moving?" While she may never have a clear answer to her questions, she can come to realize that all of these changes can contribute to her uneasiness and that moving brings about its own special stresses.

Moving forces you to negotiate a new identity with people you have never met before. People often turn to friends and family for social support during these life transitions. But after you move, you may find it difficult, if not impossible, to find support in your new location. Your new neighbors probably don't want to hear that you're having difficulty adjusting to the community they have learned to love. You may not want to tell the friends you left behind that you think you made a mistake. As a result, you face these transitions alone.

Even when multiple events are positive, they drain energy and force you to confront a new identity. Georgianna's new job was a step up for her career. "As soon as I got here, I realized my clothes wouldn't work anymore. I had to give away most of my wardrobe. It was not consistent with who I wanted to be here."

Sorting Out Your Feelings

While you may feel confused about your feelings, others will be confused about how to offer help. Many people are not even aware that stress is common during moving. When you share your experience, you may find that your listeners have a wide range of reactions. Some will say, "Moving is no big deal. People are the same all over." At the other extreme, you may find that some people are so terrified by the thought of moving that they do not want to hear about your experience: "I don't know what I'd do if I had to move. I've lived here thirty years. I'd die."

Moving is the most ambiguous of life transitions. If you lose a loved one, people know they should offer sympathy. If you get married, congratulations are in order. Yet when you announce, "I'm moving to Boise!" you may get reactions ranging from sympathy to envy to puzzlement.

Often your emotional response will be baffling to others. Edward and Helen were devoted New Yorkers. They referred to nearby Queens as the wilderness, Staten Island as Siberia. New Jersey was "out West somewhere." When Edward was transferred to Chicago in a tight job market, the couple went into mourning. "I've been exiled to Chicago!" Edward moaned. "There's no culture!" Helen exclaimed.

While some friends commiserated, others were puzzled: "Chicago is hardly a cultural wasteland." Their relatives from the country, and indeed many of their friends from New York, had no idea what they were complaining about. Yet for this couple, New York offered a lifestyle they felt they could not replace.

You are the only person who will know what you value in a lifestyle and a location, and your emotions probably won't follow a familiar formula.

Myths About Moving

The realities of moving are already daunting, but when well-meaning people exaggerate them, these problems can seem downright impossible. The following myths may be presented to you as well-meaning advice.

Myth: Moving Is Always an Occasion of Sadness

Some people will tell you to anticipate the same kind of grief you would experience after losing a loved one or going through a divorce. In her book, *The Trauma of Moving*, psychotherapist Audrey McCollum (1990) reports that several people compared moving to dying or having a limb amputated. Something they thought would always be there is gone forever, they seem to say.

Feelings of grief are common and appropriate. It is important to remember, however, that many people do not grieve a loss when they move. Some people actually feel better afterward. Jasmine told me, "I had to move before I could feel at home. I grew up in a town where nobody was interested in theater or art or classical music. It was in the Southwest. I even hated the weather. I felt better after moving north to study theater arts in college. Afterward I moved to San Francisco and it was great to feel the cold and damp. Now my husband and I live in Seattle, Washington, and I've never felt more at home."

Relocation can offer unique opportunities for personal growth. "For the first time in twenty years, I'm not just Jack's wife," said Lucille, who had moved often with her husband's military career. "Here nobody knows I'm married to a colonel. I can be me!"

Ron was transferred to a new city six months after his partner died from AIDS. The move, he said, helped heal his loss. "At first it was hard," he said, "but I knew I didn't have to be here long. So I did all kinds of things I'd never done before. I was always known as someone staid and serious, and here I've got a reputation for being kind of a party person. Who knows if I'll move again. But this is good for right now."

Eve and Boza Kahana (1983) discredited a related myth that the elderly become distressed when their environment is changed. Interviewing people who were retiring to Israel or Florida, they found many who saw their move as an opportunity to build a happy, productive future. Many saw their move as an adventure—some had even made impulsive decisions—yet the majority reported they were very happy with their new lives.

Myth: Everybody Hates to Move

Believe it or not, some people love to move around year after year. In my younger days, I thought nothing of selling my meager supply of furniture and flying across the country to start a new life. Writing in *Harper's* author Richard Ford (1992) insists that moving has given him a variety of experiences and a sense of self that most people achieve through stability. He has walked away from houses, jobs, and cars, and he says he has no regrets.

In a book long out of print, *We Sing While There's Voice Left*, the Benedictine monk Dom Hubert Von Zeller wrote an essay called simply "Restlessness." He believed that some people simply were born with souls that demanded constant motion and change. If these people settled down, he speculates, they'd become conceited and smug. For the restless, change can be a source of spiritual growth.

The research results are mixed. Some studies find no significant differences among those who moved often, while others report that those who move often are at risk for health problems. A study by Fisher and Stueve (1977) found that moving does not lead to significant psychological problems as long as people move voluntarily. What creates unhappiness, they suggest, is the lack of an alternative for people forced to move.

In fact, they point out, those who feel forced to move are no more unhappy than those who feel trapped. Many people would like to relocate but are unable to do so because they lack financial, social, or employment resources. Often the unhappiest movers are those commonly identified as the trailing spouse—the spouse who moves due to career demands of his or her partner. Those who feel dragged along by the family tend to be most resistant to moving. Those who have learned to accept and even enjoy their mobility may welcome each moving van.

Myth: If You're Not Happy Here, You Won't Be Happy Anywhere

There is no denying that some people remain perpetually unsatisfied because of some internal conflict that needs to be resolved. Recovering alcoholics will disparage those who seek what they call the geographical cure. They call it running from your problems.

The reality is that you may find yourself in a community where you just feel left out. "Okay, it's a small thing," says Mae, a Chinese-American living in the Midwest. "I feel left out when people talk about going to Europe. In my family, nobody cares about London or Paris. Our first trip is to Hong Kong or Beijing." For Herman it was holidays. "In New York, we took for granted that we'd get Jewish holidays off and many stores displayed menorahs at Christmas time. Here they just assume we're all Christians."

Your minority status may not be related to ethnic groups. You may be half of the only lesbian couple in town or the only couple in your neighborhood without children. If you're a minority of one, you may feel happier if you move to a community where you can find others like yourself. These are relevant issues to consider when you are deciding whether to move again or to remain in a new community.

Who knows, you may just get lucky when you move. In the French film *Ma Vie En Rose,* a seven-year-old boy likes to wear dresses and skirts. His parents, neighbors, and teachers recoil in horror. The child is labeled a deviant and the family is ostracized. When his father loses his job, it forces the family to move to a less affluent neighborhood, where they meet a little girl who likes to wear boys' clothes and hates dresses. The new neighbors laugh off these preferences as harmless childishness and the family finds acceptance among the new community.

Moving Tip

Hire a Car Service

When looking for housing, finding your way around a strange city can be daunting. Consider hiring a taxicab or car service for a day or a half day. The price will seem high, but it's considerably cheaper than dealing with a mistake later. Insist on a driver who knows the city. You'll see many more properties because you won't spend half an hour getting lost. As a bonus, drivers often know the areas and will share impressions ("I pick up a lawyer from here every week," "I hate coming in here because they hassle me"). The cost and quality of these services can vary a great deal. So shop around. If your company has a contract with a car service, you may qualify for better rates and service.

2

"How Does Where I Am Affect Who I Am?"

Discovering the Identity to Be Moved

People often spend more effort selecting a car than selecting a new place to live. While these priorities may seem irrational, remember that people have more guidance for buying a car than for choosing a destination. If you were buying a car you'd probably have some kind of checklist in mind. Maybe you're looking for a four-wheel-drive four-door with good gas mileage and plenty of trunk space. This checklist reflects your individual needs. If you have three children, a large dog, and a tight budget, a two-seat Porsche cannot serve as the family car.

Without a systematic way to evaluate a destination, you might find yourself with what amounts to a Porsche, when what you needed was more like a station wagon. Susan writes, "I was so excited about the job offer I didn't think about what I was getting into. I brushed aside the little voice that kept trying to warn me,

'You'll hate the place!' Logically, it made so much sense: new job, more money, and a city rated one of the ten best places to live. When I got there, I was so miserable I left the job after only two years, taking a pay cut to get away. I never realized how much I would miss my view of the mountains, or having my brothers living only twenty miles away, or even people with Virginia accents."

Susan worked with someone else's checklist—borrowing the values of a magazine that selected the ten best places for young women to live in North America. But her identity differed from the one targeted by that magazine article. For Susan, at least one of those cities was one of the ten *worst* places to live.

This chapter will help you develop your own checklist. You will look within to uncover your own identity and the way you express yourself in your community. When you know who you are, you can move confidently into social interactions and business relationships in your new community. The first step is to understand how your current residence contributes to the three building blocks of your identity: self-concept, social identity, and paper identity.

The Three Building Blocks of Identity

Your identity is a summary of who you are. Many life transitions are accompanied by a public statement of identity change. A marriage ceremony changes you into a spouse, while divorce papers signal your return to being single. The birth of a child, a graduation, the death of a loved one—all are marked by certificates and sometimes even a change of name and legal status.

A change of residence has no ceremony or certificate. You might attend a few farewell parties, apply for a new driver's license, vote in a new jurisdiction, and pay new taxes, but no formal declaration occurs. Moving can force you to revise your identity as deeply as any other life transition, yet there is no outward validation of this transformation.

Think of your identity as composed of three building blocks that are joined together: your *self-concept*, your *social identity*, and your *paper identity*. Your *self-concept* is based on the way you describe yourself, your *social identity* comes from the way you believe other people view you, and your *paper identity* comes from the cards and certificates that identify you to the government and the business world. When your identity is stable, these building blocks fit together solidly, supporting and reinforcing one another. When you move, the blocks shift and may crumble if not handled carefully. In a successful relocation you build a new identity structure that fits your new location. You might even build a more solid and more satisfying structure than the one you had before.

Your Self-Concept

When you describe yourself by a series of "I am" statements, as you did in chapter 1, you begin to verbalize your self-concept. Some parts of your self-concept are visible to the people who know you; others are known only to yourself or to a few trusted friends. Your self-concept may be expressed in roles: "I am a mother, sister, dog owner, PTA secretary, lawyer . . ." You also may define yourself by your activities: "I fix cars, paint, swim, take care of my children . . ." Some people add personal qualities to their self-concept: "I am shy, athletic, not very good at math . . ."

Your self-concept may influence your feelings about moving. Tom was raised in a house that's "always been in the family." His self-concept is largely defined by residence. Selling a house, especially an old family dwelling, would clash with his self-concept. Gwen, on the other hand, was raised in a military family and therefore thinks nothing of moving from a house to an apartment, or going from buying to renting and back again. Gwen defines herself not in terms of where she lives, but through activities she can enjoy all over the world—needlework, swimming, phone calls to her family.

Your self-concept may contain definite preferences as to where you want to live. If your self-concept incorporates prize-winning gardens, you will resist moving to a high-rise apartment in a big city; whereas if you grew up in Manhattan, you may view a house with a yard as a vast untamed wilderness.

A self-concept is not easy to change, even when it's become outdated or undesirable. I know several people who still live like graduate students as they pass their fortieth birthday, refusing to replace bricks and boards with polished wood bookcases. You may know someone who has dieted to a normal weight but still views herself as fat. Sometimes people who grow up in poverty never become accustomed to having money. Often when a self-concept changes, it will conflict with your social identity.

"But My Identity Is My Work . . ."

Are you a workaholic who will move anywhere to keep on the fast track? Too busy to think, let alone work through exercises in a book? Think again. Your family members still need to maintain their identities during the many hours you are at work. An unhappy family can become a distraction as well as a source of your own unhappiness.

Whether or not you move with a family, you may need to interact with the local community. Many people like to keep their private lives separate from the job for business reasons. You may get sick or you may find yourself in a personal crisis. Perhaps most important, your work environment will probably reflect the local culture: what people wear, what they talk about at lunch, even what hours they keep.

Karen had just accepted a promotion to be Director of Marketing Support in a district office of her national company. Chatting with her assistant one day, she was dismayed to learn that some of her new colleagues thought she was standoffish.

"People like to come in on Monday and talk about what they did over the weekend," Karen's assistant explained. "Who they saw, what they did with their families . . ." Karen came from headquarters where the culture, like the headquarters city, was more formal and distant. She began to realize that the more casual life of her new city was reflected in a more casual workplace, where people wanted a more personal relationship. Updating her social identity eventually helped her become more effective at work and develop some personal relationships as well.

Your Social Identity

Your social identity is based on how others—your friends, family, and neighbors—think of you. The mother of your son's classmate calls you at the last minute: "Can you bring extra cupcakes to the picnic?" You realize she views you as a dependable parent and perhaps even a gifted baker. Your self-concept probably incorporates these roles also. When you're settled in a community, your social identity tends to affirm your self-concept.

When you move, you meet people who do not know you. Their actions may contradict the self-concept you brought from home. Your new neighbor, handing you some cuttings, asks if you know how to plant them. You want to shout, "Dammit, I won prizes for my garden!" A discrepancy has arisen between your self-concept and your social identity.

Social Roles Play on Two Stages

When you move, your social identity is revealed through two different audiences who may not know each other. Your old friends and family know what you can do: serve as club president, anchor the bowling team, baby-sit for the kids, serve as a fourth at bridge, or carry on a knowledgeable discussion about foreign affairs. Your new acquaintances don't know you. They may think of you as a blank slate or, worse, make assumptions about who you are.

Your old friends will always remember you as a neighbor, co-worker, and friend. When you move, you no longer maintain those roles. Even when old friends are no longer part of your day-to-day world, their opinions and values can still affect your identity. In their article "Salient Private Audiences and Awareness of the Self," psychologists Mark Baldwin and John Holmes (1987) report that people can be influenced by the values of those who are important to them, regardless of whether those people are physically present or even alive. Even if you never see your old friends again, you may find yourself imagining their criticism: "Harry would laugh if he could see this puny lawn," or their praise—"Jenny would love the view of the river my new house has." Think of the times someone has said to you, "If my mother were here . . ."

Your new audience may find your identity strange, even alien or scary. A prominent psychologist told listeners at a recent American Psychological Association conference that he had experienced hostility as a child when his Italian family moved from New York to Los Angeles. His new classmates associated Italians with the Mafia and said they couldn't understand his Brooklyn accent.

Your new neighbors may be interested in aspects of your identity that you have ignored all your life. Yvonne moved to Tennessee when her husband was transferred. When she applied for office manager jobs, employers were only mildly interested in her ten years of solid experience. "What did your daddy do?" they asked. Although Helene knew that her mother was Jewish, her family was not religious and Helene grew up knowing nothing about religion. When she moved to the East Coast, she was surprised when her new friends wished her Happy Hanukkah.

If you're a divorced person or a single parent you may be especially conscious of your social identity if you move to a place where more traditional family lifestyles remain prevalent. "Being the only single parent in my new conservative neighborhood was a real learning experience," one woman said ruefully. "People seemed to think I was a fallen woman." "I'm the only man in my company who takes a turn cooking for my family," said Frank. "The other guys can stay late for meetings or work all night, but my wife works and I have to pick up the kids."

Your social identity may suddenly be very impressive in your new location. Maybe even *too* impressive. When June was promoted to district manager of her internationally known bank, she moved with her husband, Alfred, to a smaller city. Suddenly June was a local celebrity. As an African-American female—the first in her position— she received a good deal of media coverage. As a senior banking official, she wielded financial clout and served on half a dozen boards. She was also in demand as a speaker. Alfred, who had retired from his own career to pursue his artistic interests, found himself escorting his wife to social functions. June had developed a new, unsought social identity. She could no longer throw on a pair of old jeans and a sweatshirt to shop for groceries. Nearly everyone she met was a potential client. Some people were intimidated, while others were resentful. "I can never let my guard down, except at home," she says. "I am always on display."

Your Paper Identity

While your social identity represents the way you are regarded by friends and neighbors, your paper identity reflects the way you are perceived when you enter into a transaction where money or services will be exchanged. How fast can you get a loan? How easily can you rent an apartment, cash a check, borrow books from the library, or check out videos? You may develop a close relationship with your hair stylist, but she probably won't keep cutting your hair if you can't pay for her services.

Landlords, video rental stores, government agencies, utility companies, and most retail businesses do not view you as "John, the dedicated family man" or "Elena, the warm supportive friend." They relate to you based on their assessment of your ability to meet your financial responsibilities. They may display extra concern and care not because they like your delightful personality and scintillating sense of humor, but because you are a valued customer who is likely to return and spend even more money.

In today's economy, this aspect of your identity can often be assessed through pieces of paper. Your ability to engage in major financial commitments, such as a mortgage or business investment, will be based on your credit report. For most transactions, your ability to make purchases will depend on the cards you carry in your wallet: credit cards, health club membership, business cards from your employer, driver's license, frequent flyer cards, and more. Sometimes the price you pay will depend on the pieces of paper you carry with you.

Will your neighbors invite you to their barbecue? The answer depends on your social identity. Will you be able to rent an apartment, a car, a video, or a power tool? The answer depends on your paper identity. As far as these rental companies are concerned, you do not exist outside your paper identity. After you move, this identity may be weakened. Some banks in Florida will credit your deposits faster after your account has been open for six months. It may take some-time to get your new driver's license. Your frequent flyer points on Alaska Airlines will not get you an upgrade from Dallas to Chicago.

After you have lived in the same place for a while, you'll develop business relationships that require you to show fewer pieces of paper. The merchants and professionals you deal with already know your paper identity. As a newcomer, your weakened paper identity can create trouble for the other parts of your identity. You have to show a driver's license to pay by check at the grocery store; your neighbor doesn't. You have to fill out endless forms to obtain a place to live. You may begin to wonder, "Am I really the person I think I am?"

Your Identity As a Resident of . . .

Now it's time for you to discover your own unique building blocks. These exercises will help you consider your identity as a series of life-style components that are available where you happen to live. By gaining an awareness of your three building blocks, you will begin to envision your identity-based checklist. Even if you decide not to move, the insights gained from these exercises can help you plan for future contingencies.

Self-Concept Exercise
My Week in Focus

This exercise will help you understand how you express your self-concept in activities, whether alone or with others.

Keep a journal for a week. Choose an ordinary week, when you have no out-of-town visitors, holidays, or birthday celebrations. For each day, record the following:

- **Event:** What did you do? (If you are busy, record just one or two events that stood out for you each day. No event is too trivial, as long as it was important to you.)

- **Feelings:** What did you think about during the event. Did you enjoy it? dislike it?

- **Wishes:** What, if anything, do you wish were different about this event? Is there something you'd rather be doing? (This section may offer clues to a new valued identity that could be available at your future destination.)

Do not judge yourself, your activities, or your reactions. Simply write down your feelings as they occur to you.

(Note: If you are moving as a family, each member should work through all the exercises individually. Children who are old enough to write should keep their own diaries and try the other exercises as well. Expect some surprises!)

After keeping the journal you should be able to list a series of activities and interests that express your identity. To illustrate, we'll follow four people as they decide whether to move from Boston to a small town in Iowa. Although they share a common origin and destination, each person's identity blocks shape the way they evaluate their destination.

Elaine is divorced and works as a health care systems consultant. Her company wants her to manage a new branch to serve key customers. The job would advance her career significantly, but she's never lived away from the East Coast.

Harry is Asian-American and gay. He was offered a transfer to work in the agricultural division of a large corporation, a step up for his career. Having just broken off a relationship, he feels free to move but fears his personal life will be stigmatized in a small Midwestern town.

Bruce and Nancy were married two years ago and await the birth of their first child. They desperately want to move to a more rural area where they can buy a large house with a yard. Bruce, an accountant, thinks he can set up his own business in the new location. Nancy's cousin lives in Iowa and has urged them to make the move.

From Elaine's Journal:
Sunday
10 A.M.
Event: Classes at local gym: spinning! wall-climbing! so many offerings.
Feelings: I love it. It feels so state-of-the-art, and I am at home.
Wishes: It's such great weather: I wouldn't mind going on hikes now and then.

2 P.M.
Event: Painting class at local art school.
Feelings: I get to play!

"How Does Where I Am Affect Who I Am?"   33

Wishes: I'd like more time to dabble in paint.

Monday
8 A.M.
Event: Cappuccino and the *Times* at the great little place down the street.
Feelings: A highlight of the day. Gets me out of bed.
Wishes: That this place would never close!

7:30 P.M.
Event: Met friends to view new French film that just opened.
Feelings: Comfortable, familiar. I like talking about films with my friends.
Wishes: Do this more often.

Tuesday
9 A.M.
Event: Cat to vet. Luckily vet is only four blocks away—a fast cab ride.
Feelings: Glad I have a good vet—a feline specialist.
Wishes: I could walk to the vet if the cat would lose some weight.

From Harry's Journal:
Saturday
8 A.M.
Event: Hike in the country.
Feelings: Great to be outdoors again!
Wishes: I'd like to have a dog to take with me.

Monday
8 A.M.
Event: Brewed a pot of coffee to go with the muffins I made yesterday.
Feelings: Cozy! Especially on a cold morning.
Wishes: Wish I could stay home longer during the week.

7 P.M.
Event: Friends came over for pot luck and a video.
Feelings: What I like best: being with people.
Wishes: More space, bigger kitchen, bigger parties.

10 P.M.
Event: Walked home with a new friend.
Feelings: Beautiful night! Cold but clear.
Wishes: I'd like to live in the country and see the sky more often. And I'd like to meet someone new.

Tuesday
9 A.M.
Event: Cat to vet.
Feelings: Traffic is a hassle.
Wishes: Wish I could have a dog.

From Bruce's Journal:
Sunday
10 A.M.
Event: Played Basketball at the YMCA.
Feelings: Great workout.
Wishes: Improve my jumpshot.

Monday
3 P.M.
Event: Meeting at the accounting firm.
Feelings: Frustrated with my boss.
Wishes: Start my own business.

Tuesday
8 A.M.
Event: Coffee with Jim before work.
Feelings: Fun to shoot the breeze.
Wishes: Wish atmosphere at work was more like this.

From Nancy's Journal:
Sunday
3 P.M.
Event: Brunch with Jody from school.
Feelings: She's a riot!
Wishes: I'm glad I met friends at work.

Monday
12 P.M.
Event: Lunch in classroom.
Feelings: Love to spend time with these kids.
Wishes: My own kid to have fun with.

Tuesday
5 P.M.
Event: Step class at the YMCA.
Feelings: My endurance is getting good.
Wishes: Work my way up to the advanced class.

Bruce and Nancy got a surprise: their entries were almost identical. They both enjoyed going to work and eating with friends. They also both enjoyed being active—Bruce played basketball and Nancy did aerobics. When they looked closely, they realized most of their friendships came from their careers. Bruce socialized with colleagues from his accounting firm and even some former clients. Nancy had taken a temporary job teaching at an elementary school where she'd become close friends with a few other teachers. This couple knew they could thrive in a small town in Iowa—if they could earn a living at congenial jobs.

Social Identity Exercise
The Protected Witness

The Witness Protection Program offers protection to witnesses whose lives are in danger after they testify in open court. They receive new names, new occupations, and new places to live. People do not lose their identities easily, however. Some witnesses find that they cannot give up certain hobbies, activities, or lifestyle components. These traits sometimes make it possible for the "bad guys" to find these hidden witnesses, often with disastrous consequences.

Ask a friend to imagine that you have entered the Witness Protection Program. After your friend has gotten used to the idea, ask them to imagine that they wanted to track down your whereabouts. They aren't sure where you're living, so they visit locations in several cities to see if you show up. Where would they look?

Elaine's friend answered, "I'd look in theaters showing foreign films, bookstores, coffee shops, and museums!"

Harry's friend laughed: "Cookware stores! I know you like to fix gourmet meals. But you also play tennis and you like parties."

Bruce and Nancy found their friends had anticipated what they wanted: "A little house with a big yard and a swing set in the back. Bruce would be mowing the lawn. And you'd both be involved in some kind of stuff for kids."

This exercise should reinforce what you learned in the diary exercise, but there may be some surprises. If you've been telling yourself, "Well, I can live without . . . " your friend's observations may encourage you to reconsider your decision.

You can modify this exercise by asking your friend to imagine that the Witness Protection Program has assigned you to the destination you are considering. The marshals are wondering if you're going to be okay. What do they think?

When Elaine asked her friends how they thought she'd react to living in a small town in Iowa, they were startled by the question. "Crying and miserable," they said. "You're such an urban person."

Harry's friends were also discouraging: "Nobody to talk to besides your dog. No nightlife. No parties. Do they have gourmet food stores in Iowa? Won't they be bigoted?"

Nancy and Bruce were surprised by their friends' acceptance. "No big deal. We figured you guys would want to move and start a family soon."

═══ Social Identity Exercise ═══
The New Me

The place where you live represents an extension of your self-concept and also a source of real and imaginary reactions from others. How many times do people ask, "Where are you from?" How do you feel when you answer? This exercise asks you to examine your feelings about your new social identity as a resident of the new location. Here are some questions to get you started:

How will you feel driving a car with the license plate of the new state?

You are wearing a convention badge that lists you as a resident of the new city. People come up to you and say, "Oh, I see you're from . . . " What do you think? What do you say?

You are traveling on an airplane and your seatmate asks, "Where are you from?" Again, how do you feel about announcing your new residence?

You are attending a college or family reunion. People ask, "So where are you living now?" How do you feel about sharing your new lifestyle with old friends and family? Will they think you've come down in the world or will they be impressed? Will they support the new you?

You return from an overseas trip. The customs official asks, "Where do you live in the United States?"

Write down your feelings as they occur to you. Again, do not judge yourself, just write down your thoughts as they appear. You might be surprised at your reactions.

Elaine felt a sinking feeling when she thought of mounting Iowa plates on the car she would have to buy. She knew her friends would tease her if she moved to one of those small towns. She told herself it didn't matter, but she knew she loved her "big city" image. She loved saying, "I live in Boston," and showing people around.

Harry loved the idea of being from a place that nobody had ever heard of. He knew his old friends would express surprise and dismay when he announced his destination. He realized he would have to learn more about the local culture before making a final decision.

Bruce and Nancy were extremely optimistic. Both had relatives in the Midwest and had grown up in cities much smaller than Boston. Many of their friends were undergoing similar transitions, moving to the suburbs to have children. They anticipated supportive responses.

As you can see, there is a broad spectrum of possible responses. My friend Tina had the most resistance of anyone I ever met. She couldn't bear to give up her California license plates for the two years she spent in Tennessee. She flew back each year to renew her registration. In her second year, California began to require vehicle inspection. Tina managed to persuade the clerk to defer inspection for another year. By the time her car needed to be inspected, she was back on the West Coast.

Sam and Hillary had an opposite response. Sam's last assignment before retirement turned out to be Juneau, Alaska. They hated the cold weather and the isolation and having to fly thirteen hours to visit their children, but they loved telling people, "We live in Alaska." They bought sweatshirts, T-shirts, mugs, ashtrays, and other mementos—enough to start their own souvenir shop.

Paper Identity Exercise
Can I See Some ID?

This exercise will help you evaluate your financial and business identity in the destination city. You may also uncover feelings about your self-concept or social identity.

Spread your credit cards, ID cards, and membership cards on a table and look at them.

Pull out any business cards you may have collected. You may even want to search through your address book for any stores and organizations you regularly use.

Which would change or disappear if you moved? Put them into a separate pile.

Summarize your new paper identity.

Elaine wrote, "I will have a senior position in a medium-size firm in the new city. I earn well above the average income and my expenses are low. I would need a new tax preparer. I could deal with my broker long-distance. My company's reputation would help me get a loan to buy a new car. Two credit cards are issued through a local bank. It will be more convenient if I find new cards . . ." Harry was in a similar situation. For them, paper identity will not be an issue.

For Bruce and Nancy, their paper identity will take center stage. They will need to establish credit without the umbrella of a local employer. They will need to retain credit cards and any other business relationships until they can establish their credibility.

Moving Tip

The Bare-Bones Move

Want to move but can't afford a professional moving company? Don't give up.

Of course, you can rent a van or truck, but you may not want to navigate icy mountain passes in an unfamiliar heavy vehicle. Here's what you can do:

If your possessions can be packed into large cardboard boxes, you may be able to use air freight. I've moved this way from Fairbanks, Alaska, to Winnipeg, Canada, and from Philadelphia to Rochester, New York. Of course, you cannot move sofas, beds, or dressers this way, but your possessions will be moved quickly and you will be surprised at the cost. Call the freight department of any airline.

If you don't have a car, or your car is too small, look up "Automobile Transportation" in the Yellow Pages. Often you can drive someone's car to your destination city. You deposit a sum of money ($100 last time I checked) and show your driver's license. You pay gas and oil and bill the car's owners for repairs en route.

Okay, the car is packed but you have two suitcases that just won't fit. Call a national bus company. Chances are they'll haul your excess baggage at a reasonable price.

3

"Will I Still Be Me?"

Making the Right Decision

If you're thinking about moving from Boca Raton to Boston or vice versa, you probably know one place is cold and the other isn't; but you won't know much more than that until you start digging. Consumer guides don't come with a handy checklist of features that matter to you, so in order to study a new location, you have to establish your own guidelines. Can everyone in the family find employment? Will you have someone to talk to? Will the new community find you approachable? Will you be dismissed as a newcomer who didn't go to the local high school and who can't trace your roots back three generations? Or will you find fulfillment and growth soon after you move in?

In chapter 2 you learned how your residence contributes to the three building blocks of your identity. Now you'll need to discover how this identity will fit into your new location. First, you'll need to figure out what lifestyle will be available at your destination. Then you'll compare what is available with what you need. Your final step will be to develop a contingency plan to protect your most threatened identity.

Discovering What Will Be Available

Losing opportunities to express yourself means losing part of who you are. So when you research a new location, you need to investigate options to maintain the aspects of identity you value the most. Many people become anxious and stressed when they are forced to change the way they express their identity after they move to a new location. Some aspects of identity may not find expression at all: "I couldn't find a place to take a painting class"; "The high school doesn't offer a sports team"; or "I'll miss the Saturday morning farmers market."

On the other hand, you may look forward to changing your identity when you move, gaining new opportunities for self-expression, uncovering new aspects of your identity that lead to personal growth and deep satisfaction: "My daughter will be able to study ballet at a professional school"; "I won't be a minority anymore"; or "The place reminds me of where I grew up."

Now you can begin to study what's available at your destination. Visit the new location, read whatever's available, and guide your mouse through a series of websites on your computer.

Face to Face with Your Destiny

If you have an opportunity to visit your destination in person, you can begin to seek answers to two big questions:
1. What is out there?
2. How do I react to this environment?

Try to schedule a visit for at least two or three days. Be aware that midweek and weekend days will differ: a Sunday afternoon stroll may convince you that you're moving to a laid-back place with a casual lifestyle; but the same crowd shows up Monday morning in pinstripes. Use the following exercise as a guide to help you take notes.

=== Exercise ===
The Urban Anthropologist

During your visit, imagine that you are an anthropologist viewing a culture for the first time. Your job is to collect data. Here is a checklist for your own set of field notes. You don't have to follow the sequence presented here, just jot down observations as they occur to you. Feel free to come up with additional questions.

It is important that you remain objective, so do not analyze your data in the field.

People

- How do people talk? Do they speak loudly or softly? Fast or slow? Wave their hands or fold them? What words do they use over and over again? Do people seem to smile? Frown? Do you cringe at some of their attitudes? Do you laugh at their jokes? What kinds of questions do they ask you?

- Ask directions of people (ordinary people, men, women, police officers, gas station attendants). Are they helpful? Annoyed? Do you understand their answers to your questions? Does anyone stop to offer you directions without being asked?

- What do the people look like? What do they wear? Do the men's hairstyles proclaim Surfer Boy or Marine Corps? Do men wear earrings? Do women wear makeup? Jewelry? Do they color their hair?

- How do strangers react to you? Do people say hello and smile when they see you? When you stop to admire a dog or a lawn, does the owner pull back or appreciate the attention?

- Did you find it easy to talk to the people you meet? Or do you have reactions like these:

    They kept interrupting me.

    I felt like a snob, but their hair-dos were ten years out of date.

    They never talked. A conversation was like pulling teeth.

Scenery

- What is your first reaction to the scenery? Flat? Depressing? Thrilling? Stimulating? Ugly? Breathtaking?

- How do people keep their lawns (or balconies, in a city)? Focus on the two or three neighborhoods where you might want to live. Landscaped? Lawn chairs? Flamingos? Overgrown?

- Does the place seem clean? Do you feel safe?

- How do you respond to the architecture? Do you see high-rises clustered together, single-story houses with large yards, or something in between?

The place seemed so dirty! I kept wanting to wash my hands.

The town is one big strip mall. It was so depressing.

The houses seemed to be made out of cardboard. Everything was built yesterday.

Lifestyle

• Do people walk, take public transportation, or drive everywhere?

• Did you do anything you truly enjoyed? A walk in a park, stroll through a mall, drive down a scenic road? A relaxing dinner or leisurely cup of coffee?

• Do stores and restaurants stay open late and can you shop on weekends?

• What cultural and sports activities are available?

• Can you find your favorite foods here? (This point may seem trivial, but food is an important part of who we are.)

Feelings

• Often your body will telegraph important messages while you are visiting a new location. Pay attention! The body does not lie, cover up, or make excuses. Do you find yourself experiencing unusual physical symptoms?

   I was exhausted.

   People usually describe me as a dynamo, but I could barely stay awake!

   Everything was fine except when I went to dinner and everyone asked me, "How old are your kids?" I got that sinking feeling in my stomach.

• Did you find yourself missing your current home?

   When you return home, it's time to analyze your data. Call a friend or two to discuss your observations.

   Review your notes again after three or four days, and again after a week if you have more time for a decision. When you're done, keep your notes. If you decide to move after all, you will enjoy reviewing your first reactions.

If time allows, make a return trip. During your first visit, you may not meet people who can answer your questions. They may be unaware of resources in the community that are important to you. Life rarely offers you a random sample. You may meet the only six people in San Francisco who have never eaten Chinese food. If you are single, you may meet only married people with children; if married, you may come away feeling that everyone is divorced. A native Canadian once told me solemnly, "People in Canada are atheists like me."

Also, be aware that as seasons change so do lifestyles. After a job interview in South Florida, I shared my enthusiastic response with a friend who had been born and raised in Tampa. He laughed at my reaction: "You realize, of course, you were here during our very best month—April!" A summer visit to Fairbanks, Winnipeg, or Fargo will offer no clues to the life you can expect to lead during the eight-month winter.

Living Room Research

In order to get the most out of your visit, do some research before you go. Visit your local library. If you have Internet access, go online and check out information on the World Wide Web. When you return from your trip you may want to supplement your visit by conducting additional detailed research. Here are some suggestions for researching a destination without leaving home.

Surf the World Wide Web

You can find a website for nearly every corner of the world, from the smallest hamlet to the largest city. You can get information about housing prices, recreation, culture, sports, even relocation packages. You can also find the websites of local businesses, theater and film listings, museum guides, recreation facilities, airport transportation, health care facilities, and a whole lot more.

It's important that you check the date of the last update. Some sites are left alone for years at a time, while others are updated daily. This way you can make sure the information is current.

Search Online Bookstores

The Internet has online bookstores that often are more comprehensive than any library or local bookstore. Check the websites of Amazon Books (www.amazon.com) and Barnes & Noble (www.barnesandnoble.com). You may even find a book tailored to your destination. My own search turned up a particularly frank guide, *What*

Sucks about South Florida. Few local bookstores carry all these guides, but you can order them through the website or ask your local bookstore to place a special order. If you're very patient, you can even ask your library for an Interlibrary Loan.

Don't Skip Travel Guides Designed for Tourists

Some of these travel guides include information about pharmacies, coffee shops, grocery stores, health clubs, and entertainment options that will be useful for permanent residents. You may even end up guiding the locals around their own national parks, restaurants, and cultural institutions. I found a first-rate hair stylist in Philadelphia from a Frommer guidebook.

A word of caution: Books go out of date very quickly. If the local guide promises a theater with foreign films, be sure it's still in business if that's important to you. Sports teams can leave town without warning. A new shopping mall can change the entire mood of a city.

Other Resources

Write or call the Chamber of Commerce for a relocation package. The package will be biased toward members of the Chamber, but you will get a listing of business groups, retail stores, and a sense of the business climate.

The Yellow Pages of the telephone directory offer a great deal of information about the area's culture. What kind of restaurants does the city have? How many vegetarian restaurants? Steakhouses? Fast food places? How many hair salons? Psychologists? Health clubs? Sports bars? Adult entertainment centers? You can learn a lot about the local culture by studying what kind of businesses a city supports. You may want to make some calls to see what these firms have to offer—or if they're still in business.

Defining Where You Belong

Now you can put together your own checklist and evaluate the new destination. Nothing is too trivial. A writer who lives in Los Angeles once told a group about a job interview in Houston: "I got off the plane. Where was the ocean? Where was the cappuccino? I couldn't live there!" And he didn't.

=== Exercise ===
I Gotta Be Me

What do I need to be me? Begin by listing what's important to your self-concept. Consult the My Week in Focus exercise from page 31 for some ideas.

Here are some examples:

- Opportunities for spouse to work
- Favorite sports team
- Food to cook Chinese, Thai, Mexican meals from scratch
- My own house with a yard
- Housekeeping services
- Hair/nail salons
- Health club with Nautilus machines
- Public library with big mystery section
- Cappuccino bar where I can hang out
- Access to the ocean or mountains
- Sushi bar
- Places to hear jazz
- Place to study piano
- Opportunity to sing in a choir
- Baby-sitters
- Churches of a special denomination
- Absence of traffic noise: no sirens interrupting my dinner!
- Easy to keep a car
- Driving in snow or mountains

When you are done, look over your list. Ask yourself, "What *must* be there?"

Place a star beside any item that is non-negotiable. The item may be non-negotiable because it is necessary to your physical or mental health. It may be non-negotiable just because it is important to you.

Some factors may cause you to block a destination altogether. Here are some examples:

My skin can't handle the dry climate in the Southwest.

I have a deaf child who needs special schools.

My child's sports team is coached by a professional player.

I need to see the ocean.

My parents are getting older and we need to live within driving distance.

My wife will go crazy if she doesn't work.

How Will People React to You in the Community?

Psychologists believe that people respond to others with a general "approach" or "avoid" orientation. Review notes from your visit. Did you find yourself wanting to approach or avoid the people you met? Did they approach or avoid you?

Your social identity will evolve from the way you believe others respond to you. Did people respond to you with openness and warmth? Or did they avoid eye contact, suggesting they felt uncomfortable with you? Did you feel accepted, or did you find yourself sharing the thoughts of the woman who said, "I felt they looked at me like they were trying to find something wrong with me."

It is very difficult to assess threats to your social identity without a face-to-face visit. You can try to find people like yourself by studying what activities seem to be available.

Local Newpapers

Skim through newspapers (especially weeklies) to see what activities are being offered. Also check the Yellow Pages. If there are many activities you would enjoy, chances are that a sizable segment of the population enjoys them as well.

Local Organizations

If you belong to an alumni association from college, a fraternity, or other social group, ask for names of members in the new location. Those who agree to be listed with a membership office are usually willing to talk to newcomers. Your common background allows you to make a comparison: "How is this city like our college town?"

═ Exercise ═══════════════════════════════
What's The Difference?

A chart is a good way to help you evaluate your chosen location.

Make three columns. In the first column list the things that are important to you. (You should consult the list you made in the "I Gotta Be Me" exercise on page 45.) At the top of the second column write "What's here," and above the third, "What's there." Now take the important qualities one by one and compare what you have now to what you would have if you moved to your chosen location.

Then consult the "My Week in Focus" exercise on page 31. Are there any wishes you made that seem important to you? List the wishes in the first column and then compare the likelihood of your wishes coming true where you are now with the likelihood of them coming true in your new location.

Elaine, the urbanite, made a chart like this one:

What's Important	*What's Here*	*What's There*
my morning cappuccino!	lots of good places	one place, an hour's drive
getting my hair done	a sophisticated salon	I'd drive to Chicago every six weeks
saying, "I live in Boston"	I feel good	"I live in Iowa?!"
my cats	no problem	no problem
getting around	I walk everywhere	I'd need a car
What I Wish		
more outdoors on weekends	possible, but difficult	easy!
more time for art lessons	access but no time	time but less access to lessons

Harry's chart looked like this:

What's Important	*What's Here*	*What's There*
my cat	just a cat	I could get a dog!
cooking for friends	a little cramped, but I can do it	lots of room, but it will be hard to find friends
being outdoors	hard to get to country	easy!

my social life	night life, friends, groups	I don't know who to ask
What I Wish		
house with yard	apartment with terrace	yes—affordable, too!

Bruce and Nancy's chart looked like this:

What's Important	*What's Here*	*What's There*
a big house	a small apartment	lots of good houses
safe place to live	depends on neighborhood	no sirens!
ties to business community	a solid network, alumni association	start from scratch

After completing the charts, put them away for a while. Even if your decision has a deadline, try to give yourself at least forty-eight hours. Forget about moving and do something else altogether. Solutions to complex problems often emerge only after you stop thinking about the problems.

Protecting Against Identity-Threatening Surprises

Good planning can help you manage your move and protect your shifting identity. Yet even the best plans can go astray through no fault of your own. Sandra, a vegetarian, was relieved to learn that her new town had two health food stores, one of which offered take-out deli service. Right after she moved, one went out of business and the other changed ownership.

You can't plan for every contingency, but you can develop what business people call "worst-case scenarios." When you are moving, you need to evaluate other possible identity losses. You can come up with worst-case scenarios by focusing on whatever block of identity is most critical for you. A worst-case scenario can be expressed as a contingency question: "What if this happened to me?" If you develop answers to the contingency question before you move, you will be ready to protect whatever part of your identity feels threatened. Continuing with the examples, Elaine is most concerned with self-concept, Harry with social identity, and Bruce and Nancy with paper identity. Each will develop a worst-case scenario.

Protecting a Threatened Self-Concept

For Elaine, the contingency question was: "What if I can't find activities that I enjoy doing, that make me feel more like me?" Elaine's worst-case scenario involved losing access to creative, fulfilling activities. "I don't watch much television," she says, "and I am definitely not a football fan."

To answer this question, Elaine reviewed her My Week in Focus exercise. She planned getaways: long weekends when she could fly back to Boston. To assure herself that trips were practical, she resea-rched the local airports, highways, and train schedules. She realized she could arrange with friends for telephone calls and frequent visits. She could try to find a therapist who would be willing to offer telephone consultations in a familiar Boston accent. She decided to enroll in correspondence courses.

After sharing her ideas with some friends, Elaine decided she would take another precautionary step. Companies sometimes abandon people in places that are off the beaten track. After eighteen months had passed, Elaine would make sure her résumé was in the hands of several search firms. She would spread the word among her professional networks. Within two years, she could be back in Boston.

Protecting a Threatened Social Identity

For Harry, the question was, "What if others do not seem to respond to the real me—the person I know I am?" Harry's worst-case scenario involved not only isolation, but also prejudice and overt hostility. Unlike Elaine, Harry knew he could preserve his self-concept through activities: hiking, cooking, talking to friends long-distance.

Harry decided that he needed a local support group to provide positive reinforcement. Unless he had some definite opportunities for support, he would not move. He also created an emergency fund in case his new situation became unbearable. That way he could return to Boston or another city he knew offered a social life he enjoyed.

Protecting a Threatened Paper Identity

Bruce and Nancy knew they would enjoy the social life of a small town, but were concerned about developing business and financial relationships. Their contingency question was, "What if we start a business that fails?" They also wondered, "What if we run out of money before the business gets off the ground?"

Bruce decided to investigate jobs he could obtain as a last resort: house-painting, temporary accounting work, or even part-time teaching. Nancy figured she could get another temporary teaching job in her new location. If they found themselves financially strapped, Nancy could return to teaching. Her salary and benefits could be used to buy more time for Bruce to develop his business.

When Employment Creates Your Paper Identity

If you move with a job, your paper identity will be established as you move. But what happens if you lose the job? Kevin, a young salesperson with a computer firm, was moved to New Jersey from Minneapolis six months after being hired. Six months later he was laid off. He had a one-year lease on his apartment and few contacts in New Jersey.

What could Kevin have done to plan for this worst-case scenario?

He could have negotiated a contract before accepting a transfer. If he were moving to an isolated one-company town, he could have made a strong case for some kind of agreement to take effect if he were laid off.

If he had good contacts in Minneapolis, he could have retained some ties to the city. Some people rent their houses or sublet their apartments for a year, taking temporary accommodations until they can size up the long-term potential of a new job.

Another possibility would have been to maintain an emergency fund that would allow Kevin to move back if things went badly.

The Thinnest Identity: Moving Without a Job or a Business

People often are tempted to quit their jobs and start over someplace new. By moving without a job, you take risks with your social identity. A common introductory question is, "What do you do?" You may also find your self-concept is threatened when you have to answer, "I'm looking for a job." Your paper identity can be especially troublesome. Without an employer, you may find yourself facing skepticism from telephone companies, landlords, and financial institutions.

It's not easy to assess a new job market. Ralph had managed jewelry stores in Houston for twenty years when he and his wife decided to move to Philadelphia. Their teenage son wanted to study at a prestigious music conservatory, but was too young to live alone. Ralph's wife had never worked and they found few jewelry stores in Philadelphia, none of which were hiring. The family saw their savings dwindle as they tried to find a place to live that would accommodate four people and one medium-size dog.

You cannot expect that a particular set of professional skills will be in demand. Arlene is a physician and found it difficult to find a job in some provinces of Canada; a shortage of hospital facilities restricts the number of physicians allowed to practice. The old standbys—teaching, social work, library science—have become crowded fields, often unionized, with long waiting lists.

Some people take the leap and land safely through a combination of luck and planning. Most of them have taken some or all of the following actions:

They protected the identity created by work. They lined up a job—even a temporary job—before moving. Those who worked freelance lined up at least one client before moving.

They defined their occupational self-concept flexibly. They were willing to wait tables, paint houses, or work as temporary secretaries if necessary.

They worked in a skilled trade that was in demand. Some jobs like carpentry, plumbing, auto mechanic, and computer repair are in demand almost everywhere.

They guaranteed a strong social identity through relatives and close friends living in the area. These contacts could serve as references and also introduce them to the local networks.

They established a paper identity ahead of time. A few phone calls allowed them to identify what they would need to set up a home and establish local credit.

"I'm Open to Change."

Your new residence may open doors to possibilities you never dreamed of. "I never thought I'd care about the beach," said a new Florida resident, "but I have to admit I enjoy walking along the ocean and seeing all the sand and the palm trees."

However, if you base your decision on change, you may be in for some surprises. Elaine might tell herself, "Okay, I can't get the culture I'm used to, but I can get into something new. Cross-country skiing sounds terrific." Yet if Elaine has never seen a pair of skis up close, she may find herself experiencing yet another frustration. If she chooses a teacher who turns out to be unsupportive, she may find herself unable to learn even if she has the skills and coordination.

Some activities turn out to have an unexpected downside. "Bird-watching sounds like fun," said Lawrence, until he discovered that this hobby requires gallons of insect repellent as well as infinite patience.

There is always some risk in basing a new identity on a new interest. On the other hand, if you know yourself well, you may be able to fulfill a lifetime dream. Miguel had always wanted to fly airplanes, but not in the New York metropolitan area where he lived. When he accepted a transfer to Kansas City, Miguel immediately signed up for lessons. "You're a natural!" the instructor told him. If Miguel moves again, he will insist that his new location support his new lifestyle.

Did They Stay or Did They Go?

So what happened to the four people who were deciding whether or not to relocate from Boston to a small city in Iowa?

Elaine decided not to move. She had earned pension rights at her job and had put away some savings. Elaine learned a great deal from the decision-making process, however. After doing the exercises, she began to pay more attention to her lifestyle needs. She realized she needed to be in a big city, yet she had chosen a field where many jobs were located in small towns. She shuddered as she reviewed her emotional reaction to the small Midwestern city: "I'll never make that mistake again!"

Elaine realized that a large part of her identity was based on living in Boston. What she needed was some kind of insurance that she would be able to live where she wanted. She decided to start an emergency fund, in case she had to support herself during a long period of unemployment. She met with a career counselor to explore possibilities that would let her stay in Boston even if she lost her job. She began to think of starting her own business.

Harry decided to move to the small town. Working with his worst-case scenario, he decided that he could move back to Boston after six months if he found that he was truly miserable. He moved money into an emergency fund in case he had to choose between his job and his city.

Harry also planned getaways. He spent lots of time researching the location on the Internet. He realized that he had easy access to larger cities by train, highway, and air. He planned to visit friends and hang out in places where he could "just be me, out in the open."

Most important, Harry discovered a large university located ten miles away. Searching the university's website, he discovered that students and faculty were drawn from all over the country, even the world. The university had a Gay/Lesbian Association and an Asian Student Association—both potential sources of support groups.

Harry decided he would live in the university town, even though his commute would be slightly longer than he wished. Realizing he faced some lonely weekends, he adopted a dog and signed up for obedience classes, where he met lots of people who responded positively to his new identity as "dog owner."

Harry fulfilled the wishes that supported his self-concept. While he gave up some important elements of his lifestyle, he now had a house with a yard and a dog. Also, because he planned carefully, he carried himself with self-confidence and self-acceptance. By the end of six months, Harry had invested the emergency fund in a new car. He knew he could survive in his new location until the company was ready to send him back to Boston.

Bruce and Nancy also decided to move. Bruce felt he could always paint houses or work for a temp agency if the family bank account dropped to the danger level. Nancy took a course that trained her to do medical transcriptions at home. By writing transcriptions, she could provide additional income after the baby came.

Bruce decided he needed a strong paper identity, as well as a strong social identity, in order to network on behalf of his business. Although working as a house painter might be fun, it would not contribute to his long-term business success. He decided to search for a job that would last at least six months.

Bruce and Nancy also realized that they were at a stage in their life when moving made sense. They would be able to put down roots in the community as their children grew.

Internet Moving Tip

Searching the Web

1. Go to your favorite search engine. I use www.yahoo.com to select specific sites rather than browse by categories.

2. When prompted for keywords, type the name of the city or town you are searching. If you are searching for a small town, such as Danville, include the state.

3. You will probably find yourself at a site sponsored by the Chamber of Commerce or another local organization. You will nearly always have the option to click on names of businesses as well as options for sports, culture, and entertainment. You will also find maps and airport information.

4. Your search will probably generate the name of the local newspaper. If not, return to the search engine and modify your keyword search to include the word "newspaper." Nearly every newspaper website offers a classified advertising section. Use this section to browse your housing options. The local newspaper can be a gold mine of information. Has there been a major crime wave? A fight over real estate taxes? A rising economy? Often you can search by keyword for articles in past issues, usually described as archives. You may have to pay a small fee for retrieving each article. The archives will be especially useful if you have specific questions. For instance, suppose you have learned that Ivy Vine School is a good place to enroll your children. A search of the archives may turn up articles about the school's changing ownership, a lawsuit against the school by an angry parent, or a list of local scholarship winners.

5. Most search engines include a Yellow Pages section. With Yahoo, for example, you can click "Yellow Pages" on Yahoo's home page. You will be prompted for names of cities. After selecting your city, you can choose categories of businesses to view. For example, suppose you wanted to find a cat sitter in Fort Lauderdale, Florida. Typing "pet sitters" as a category would generate lists of boarding kennels as well as sitters who have listings in the Yellow Pages.

PART 2

Making the Big Move

4

"I Don't Want to Leave the Good Stuff Behind"

The Separation Phase

You've decided to move. Maybe you've chosen the fast track in Boston, or perhaps a beachside retirement in Florida. It could be a farm in a small town nobody's heard of. Now that you've made the decision, you have some time before you begin packing. You may have two days, three weeks, or as long as six months.

You are now entering the first stage of your transition: separating from your identity. In order to make a smooth start it is important that you take stock of your present situation. You can divide this process into four steps:

1. Acknowledging your present identity
2. Acknowledging your grief
3. Developing rituals to say good-bye
4. Building the foundation for your new identity

Step One: Acknowledge Your Present Identity

As you begin to embark on a new identity, take some time to appreciate the person you have been in your soon-to-be-former location. You need to look at all three building blocks and acknowledge how each has been defined for you. You began this process in part 1, when you discovered the identity to be moved. Now, you will be able to draw on your work in the earlier exercises as you focus on the parts of your identity you will be leaving behind.

Acknowledge Elements of Place in Your Self-Concept

Russell Belk (1988) has suggested that certain places and possessions are so critical to an individual's identity that they can be considered part of the self. Dr. Belk has developed a concept, *the extended self*, to explain these ties. The extended self can include possessions such as clothing, furniture, and cars, as well as larger elements of the environment.

For a dyed-in-the-wool New Yorker, the skyline may be part of the extended self. For those who identify with the West Coast, they may feel incomplete without access to the ocean. Bob, who was raised in Colorado, identifies with mountains. "Real mountains," he adds, "not the little hills of Pennsylvania or Kentucky."

═ Exercise ═
Landmarks of the Extended Self

If you drew a picture of "My Home Now," what landmarks and landscape would you include? How is each element a part of who you are? You may want to refer to the exercises in the previous chapters.

Activities also help you express your self-concept. Eleanor was newly widowed and had lived and worked in New York City all her life. When she retired, she decided to move closer to her family in North Carolina. After moving, Eleanor began to realize how much she could do in the city. "In New York, you can just drop in on a museum or see the latest foreign films," she said. "I'll miss strolling down Madison Avenue, checking out the designer shops."

Hank loved to jog around a small lake near his Seattle home. When he considered moving to Michigan, he couldn't imagine beginning each day without his run. On clear days, he could see Mount Rainier in the background, framed by the evergreen trees that grow all over the city. Hank even brought bread to feed the ducks as he warmed up. He recognized other joggers, although they rarely exchanged more than a quick wave as they sped by one another. Hank tried to reassure himself that most towns have lakes or rivers with jogging paths, but he knew it wouldn't be the same. Among other things, he suspected that in Michigan it would be too cold to jog in December.

Remember how Elaine began each day in Boston with a cappuccino and croissant at her local bakery. The staff recognized her as a regular. She would arrive early in order to grab her favorite table. Nobody ever bothered her if she dawdled over the *Boston Globe* on a crowded morning.

Exercise
Activities of the Extended Self

What activities are included in your self-concept? Which are the Real You? Again, you may want to refer to the exercises in the previous chapters.

Acknowledge Your Social Identity

Most people take social identity for granted. They're often unaware of how their identity is reinforced and strengthened through interactions with others.

"I am a fanatic weight-lifter," said Tim, a banker facing a move from Atlanta to Chicago. "I come to the gym every day after work. A group of guys who train here all go out afterward and have a beer. It's a tight group. I won't find that in Chicago, at least not for a long time. It took years to build up this group."

Exercise
Introduce Yourself

Think of some occasions when you introduced yourself to someone you met at a party, a business meeting, even on an airplane.
• How did you describe yourself?

- How did you feel saying, "I'm from . . ."
- How did the other person react to you?

> *Someone said, "I've always wanted to live there."*
> *They looked shocked.*
> *They seemed to sneer.*
> *They thought Kalamazoo sounded funny.*

Now think of at least three occasions when you interacted with people you know well in your present city. How did the interactions support your self-concept?

> *She wanted to know if I'm still singing with the choir.*
> *He asked me to head another committee.*

Acknowledge Your Paper Identity

Are there any coffee shops or restaurants where you don't have to order because they know what you want? Do any stores treat you as a special customer? "Most people don't think of the library as a service business, but the librarian knows I love science fiction. As soon as I walk in the door, she tells me what's come in lately."

How do local businesses respond when you ask, "Will you take my check?" Do you receive special privileges? For example, my veterinarian will always find a cage to board the cat over the holidays. Even if I call at the last minute, they don't make me pay the late fee.

═ Exercise ═
My Business

Make a list of the local businesses you patronize frequently. Make note of any special treatment you get from the people who work there. How do these local business relationships give you support?

Step Two: Acknowledge Your Grief

As you say good-bye to your current residence, you will probably experience some grief. Leaving a place you love can be as painful as getting a divorce or mourning the death of a close friend. As you prepare to depart, the following insights may help you deal with these feelings.

Your grief is legitimate. In his book, *Death in the Midst of Life,* Jack Kamerman (1986) notes that many life events are grieved as deeply as a death in the family, yet we lack rituals to validate this grief. As a result, people are often reluctant to acknowledge their feelings. They find that their friends and family do not know how to extend sympathy and help. You may grieve losses that seem small to others: an apartment, a garden you tended for years, even a pastry shop down the street. All these losses are important; allow yourself to experience your feelings.

Dr. Michael Mayo, who I interviewed by phone, has counseled grieving clients and studied grief in organizational settings. He emphasizes that "People don't appreciate or find support for the little things. You think, 'I'm being a baby. I really miss the place where you get a good sundae, or the hardware store that had all the doodads you needed for the house and couldn't find anywhere else.'

"Yet," says Dr. Mayo, "these little things are irreplaceable. You won't find the place where you got that great sundae. You won't find that helpful man in the hardware store, the one who told you stale jokes while he found what you needed. We've over-prepared so many times for the big stuff, but we need to give legitimacy to these little things, too. The subtle nuances create our experience."

The most important part of dealing with your grief is to acknowledge your feelings. When you move, you may find yourself buried in detail, organizing your house, packing your belongings, dealing with paperwork hassles, changing addresses, and more. Make sure you take the time to acknowledge how you feel about leaving all this behind. For many people, the simple recognition of these feelings can unleash a great deal of stored-up energy. Denial comes at a major cost. Consider grief work as an investment in efficiency.

People deal with grief in many ways. Some express sadness by crying. Others may find release in physical activity, talking to others, or simply keeping busy. Some people work with meditation, visualization, or dream images. Some people use a combination of these methods.

You and your family members may grieve differently, so respect each other's methods. Whatever your style, you need to acknowledge the pain. You can't work through grief if you don't allow yourself to feel it.

"I Can't Wait to Leave!"

At the same time, you may find you have little reason to grieve if you're genuinely glad to get going. "I enjoyed living here in Cleveland," says John, "but this city was only one more stop along the way. I don't feel anything special for the city so I won't bother saying good-bye. I'll probably stay in touch with a few people, but it's no big deal."

Laura's feelings were a bit more negative: "I hated, absolutely hated, living in Philadelphia. I feel like I'm being paroled from prison."

If you're moving away from a bad situation, your good-byes will be different. Your situation resembles the person who leaves an abusive relationship. You feel that a place, not a person, has wounded you. You need time to recover from the experience. You may benefit from talking to a therapist or reading books that help you gain insights into your feelings.

Healing is a slow process and people heal at their own speed. The saying "Time heals all wounds" does not work for everyone. Forgiveness may take even longer. Some grief counselors recommend that people strive not for forgiveness, but for acceptance and acknowledgment. The following exercise may help you begin to deal with these issues.

═ Exercise ════════════════════════════
Let Me Out of Here!

Are you relieved to be moving? Do you find yourself thinking, "Thank goodness I'm out of here!" It's often difficult to realize how you have learned and grown from living in a hostile environment. Get a piece of paper and answer the following questions.

1. What are the negatives about your current residence? List as many as possible.

   Angela found fifty negatives: house needed repairs, real estate agent lied about property, garden wouldn't grow, neighbors left nasty notes in mailbox, and that was just the beginning.

2. What would you do if you were faced with the same problems in a new place?

   Angela realizes she now has important questions to ask her real estate agents. She plans to take a much closer look at the garden. And before she buys a house—or even rents for a year—she wants to meet some neighbors.

3. What have you learned from your experiences? Recognize that you may need time to appreciate these lessons.

   Angela has learned where she can get advice about major decisions that involve large sums of money. She realizes she can stand up to people who defraud her. Most important, she has learned that she can survive on her own, in a strange town, even when she's forced to deal with crises.

4. Have these lessons broadened your self-concept?

   Angela realizes she has become a more businesslike, confident person. When she describes herself now, she says, "I am independent and realistic."

Step Three:
Design Farewell Rituals

A great way to acknowledge your grief is to plan small ceremonies to say good-bye to the people and places you are leaving behind. By dedicating some time to these important parts of your life, you can enjoy them one last time and start the process of letting them go.

Exercise
What Goes and What Stays

Review the lists you made earlier in this chapter.
What will you leave behind?

- Places

_____

_____

- Possessions

_____

_____

- Activities

_____

_____

• Business relationships

_____

_____

What will you miss about those places, landmarks, and activities?

Hanging out and talking to people after a run.

The view from my window: I could see the river.

_____

What Can You Take with You?

Before saying good-bye, be sure you have no choice. Do you really have to give up this possession? For example, pets can be especially meaningful, yet many people assume they won't find housing or fear the pet won't adjust. Often they are saddened to realize they made the decision too hastily. When I talk to people who are determined to keep their large dog or their three cats, they say things like: "Sometimes you have to compromise: maybe you pay a little more or you don't get your first choice place. But it's worth it! Pet-friendly places are also people-friendly."

Of course, you can't carry a skyline or a house, but you can bring souvenirs and symbols that keep those memories alive. Just before I left Philadelphia, I bought two paintings of Rittenhouse Square from an artist who had exhibited at an art show. I don't expect the paintings to increase greatly in value, but they bring back memories of Philadelphia as an art center and I remember how much I enjoyed walking around those places depicted in bright colors on the canvas. When people see these paintings in my office, they sometimes share their own experiences of Philadelphia.

Joseph, an avid gardener, carefully picked cuttings to take to his new house. He knew the soil conditions and temperature would require him to design a totally different type of garden, but he planned to set up some window boxes and transplant some of the hardier specimens.

Some people refuse to give up aspects of their paper identity— their ties to service providers. Karen returned to her favorite hair stylist in Louisville, Kentucky, after she moved to Atlanta. Tony found a reason to return to Syracuse every six months to visit his dentist. "He knows me and doesn't bug me," he shrugged.

Plan a Farewell Ritual for People and Places You Leave Behind

In her book *True North,* Jill Ker Conway describes taking leave of her house in Toronto, where she had spent several significant years. During her time in Toronto, she built a solid foundation for her marriage, learned to love many customs of Canada, and rose from an entry-level assistant professorship to a university vice-presidency.

Dr. Conway does not describe her actions as a ritual, but her intense awareness of her experience can serve as a model for others who are leaving a place they have learned to love. Her husband had gone ahead. She loaded the car and packed some especially valuable items that were not entrusted to the moving company. She drove around the lake one last time and began driving toward Massachusetts and her new job as president of Smith College.

Other people develop more deliberate rituals. Here are some examples:

Make the last one special. Be aware of the last run around the lake, workout in the gym, picnic in the park, shopping trip to the mall.

Drink a glass of wine in your favorite place. Invite friends to join you who have shared this special place.

Spend five minutes in silence. You can spent the time saying good-bye.

Listen to your favorite music. You can wear headphones if others are nearby.

Buy something to commemorate your experience. A memento can bring back memories you thought were lost forever.

Bid Farewell to Your Consumer Relationships

When you have spent time in a place, your consumer relationships may take on a personal quality. Even if you don't become friends, these people have helped your life flow more smoothly, and you will miss the unique way they have provided their services.

Saying good-bye to service providers—doctors, lawyers, hair stylists, bankers—can feel like part of a ritual. Researchers Linda Price and Robin Higie asked people how they dealt with these professional connections when they moved away. Nearly everyone they interviewed mentioned that they had made some kind of farewell appointment. Some felt like they were leaving good friends behind.

Many asked for recommendations for finding replacements in their new locations. When saying good-bye, experienced movers often ask for records instead of recommendations. You may be surprised to learn what records can be taken with you: the formula for your hair color, your dog's medical history since puppyhood.

You can't take these services with you, but you can do the next best thing: leave open the option for a return visit or two. Getting a second opinion from a familiar resource may be expensive, but if you need reassurance you should get it from a source you trust. With some service providers, you may be able to conduct business by phone, fax, express mail, or e-mail. Some therapists now offer counseling by telephone.

With this said, it is also important to realize that your main connections with your service suppliers is a professional one even if you feel personally involved. Your new hair stylist may be better able to deal with a drier climate or a more sophisticated look that you need. Your new accountant will know the state and city tax laws. You should feel no qualms about changing practitioners when you move. An ethical professional will cooperate fully, sometimes even refusing to continue service in order to allow you to move on.

Step Four: Build the Foundation for Your New Identity

When you're working to acknowledge your feelings for the home you are leaving behind, you have the benefit of being familiar with this place; you've lived in it for some time. When you turn to face the future, things are much more mysterious. You need to start planning for a future that is largely unfamiliar. But how can you prepare for the unknown?

Plan for Fear

While many people experience grief during a move, many also experience anxiety, fear, and even panic. Panic can be viewed as the flip side of grief. When you grieve, you acknowledge the reality of a loss that has already taken place. When you feel fear, you assign reality to a loss that may happen in the future. Admitting your fear can be even more difficult than admitting your grief. Yet fear represents a realistic response to a situation that is not entirely in your control. "I feel as if I'm walking a plank," one person told me. "Maybe when I get to the end I'll go down with a crash."

You can't avoid every disaster, but you can learn how to cope with stress before it overpowers you. When you're caught in a crisis, you won't feel like heading off to the bookstore to buy a book about coping. You need to be prepared before the anxiety strikes.

In their book, *Thoughts and Feelings: Taking Control of Your Moods and Your Life,* McKay, Davis, and Fanning (1997) offer a series of what they call *coping statements.* When people feel scared, their thoughts often jumble together, and fearful thoughts reinforce each other. By preparing calm, reassuring statements, you can avoid this cycle. Some examples from *Thoughts and Feelings* (p. 132) include the following:

- Let go and relax.

- I have time to prepare.

- I've done my best. I accept whatever happens.

- I've survived this before.

You can come up with your own coping statements:

- Whatever happens, I know I can cope.

- I can deal with this.

- I can face the future with confidence.

I had a vivid firsthand experience with panic as I was writing this book. I had arranged to buy a car from a reliable mechanic. I planned to drive my new car to my new home. Ten days before the day the moving van was due to pull up to my front door, the mechanic stopped returning my calls. It was as if he'd disappeared off the face of the earth. After four days without hearing from him, I was thoroughly anxious, frazzled, and, yes, panicked. The airlines would not take my cats in ninety-degree weather. I had to drive, and now I had no car.

How would I get to Florida? What would I do for transportation after I got there? I used coping statements to deal with the immediate panic: "Let go and relax; I have time to prepare; I can deal with this." When I calmed down, I started planning with a clear head. I looked into alternate transportation. I found I could rent a car or get a drive-away and then buy another car when I arrived in Florida. I skimmed through a guide to car-buying in case I had to make a fast purchase in a new city. When the mechanic finally called back, it turned out there were problems with the title to the car. My backup plan got me through the crisis: I drove down in a rental car and bought a new car as soon as I arrived.

=== Exercise ===
I Can Cope

Write three coping statements now.
If they don't feel right for you, rework them until they do. You should feel stronger just reading the words. They will be ready when you need them.

Plan for Moving Day

If you're scared of what's ahead, you may have trouble putting a name to your fears. At this stage, you can choose to engage in what psychologist Lisa Aspinwall (1997) calls proactive coping. Most forms of coping deal with an event that has occurred or will definitely occur. In contrast, proactive coping deals with an event that may or may not occur. Often successful proactive coping is difficult to detect because a painful event is averted entirely. When you install a burglar alarm, you probably prevent attempted break-ins, but you will never know how many.

You may not be able to avoid the move, or certain unpleasant aspects of a move, but you may be able to deflect some of your fears. Eileen had never heard of proactive coping, but she knew she did not want to drive in hazardous weather conditions. She was driving from Syracuse, New York, to New Jersey in January. When negotiating with her new employer, Eileen added a special request: "If there's a blizzard on the highway, I may be delayed in arrival." Eileen's new boss, relieved that she wasn't calling to say she'd changed her mind about coming, agreed at once. If he hadn't, Eileen would have reconsidered her options. She could fly or take a train to Newark, arranging for local transportation from there. She might even have decided she didn't want to work for a company that took a hard line about driving through blizzards.

Eileen's story had a happy ending. Eileen drove on dry roads all the way to Princeton Junction, missing a blizzard by hours. Even more important, Eileen had replaced a potential source of worry with a new feeling of control.

Many advisors encourage people who move to develop a timetable for the thirty days before the actual date of the move. Some books listed in the appendix can be used to help you devise checklists that can be turned into timetables. You will find a number of benefits if you invest the time and come up with a schedule. Among other things, you can begin to plan for your worst nightmares.

Exercise
What Could Possibly Go Wrong?

Write a list of things that could go wrong with your move. Be realistic but also don't be afraid of melodrama. Sometimes the worst can happen.

For example:

The car gets stolen.

The car breaks down and takes a week to repair.

I feel lonely after I move.

The moving van is late and we have to live with an empty house.

The moving van gets stolen and we never see our possessions again.

Allow the list to sit for a day or two, longer if your move is not imminent.

Add more items as they occur to you.

Now list the events in order of severity. Obviously, this is not an objective standard. An event that seems trivial to one person will seem serious to another. Nor do you have to be rational. The odds that your move will be disrupted by a Florida hurricane or a California earthquake are very small. Yet if you are stressed, you may find yourself worrying about such unlikely events. If you accept your fears, you will have more energy to deal with the more mundane crises that are almost certain to occur. Do not judge yourself. Be honest.

Now you can begin to work through these items starting with the item labeled "most severe."

In order to work through these worries, we'll follow a plan based on Aspinwall's recommendations in an article that appeared in *Psychological Bulletin* in 1997. The basic steps are to define the problem, review your resources, and then take action.

For example, suppose your largest concern is, "Unable to use my car the last week for running errands." First, define the problem. Ask yourself, "How does my car run? What is the incidence of automobile theft in my neighborhood?"

Once you have a clear picture of what you are facing, you should review your resources. Can you rent a garage? Can you arrange a tune-up? What resources will be available if the car becomes unavailable? For example, "Will my new employer pay for a rental car as part of my moving expense? If not, what kind of car can I afford to rent at the last minute? Can I make arrangements to borrow a car from my brother-in-law across town?"

Take action! Call rental car companies. Call your mechanic. Call the brother-in-law.

Plan for Being a Newcomer

"Feeling at home means knowing how to find things and make them work," concludes psychotherapist Audrey McCollum, who interviewed dozens of people for her book *The Trauma of Moving*. While conditions may change unexpectedly, knowing what to expect can build confidence. Airline pilots study maps of airports before they land; ship captains study ocean currents; actors walk around the new stage. When you move, you will not have access to a map or chart of your new lifestyle. You need to draw your own, using as much information as you can get, and then anticipate how you will chart your own course.

When you move you will find yourself assuming new roles in your community and leaving old roles behind. You may have to modify a familiar role to fit your new situation, or even experiment with roles that you are uncomfortable with. It's all part of discovering your new identity.

=== Exercise ===
A Day in Your New Life

You are going to imagine your life after you've moved.

Relax for a few minutes. Close your eyes if it helps you concentrate.

Picture yourself in your new life. You could be just waking up or out on the town; maybe you're at work. Just pick a place and begin.

- What do you see yourself doing? Is this a familiar role for you?

- What familiar roles might come in handy in your new location? How will these roles be different now that you are a newcomer.

- What new roles might you be taking on?

- What problems might you encounter? How will you deal with these problems? Could you have avoided them?

When you are done, write down any insights. You might want to look back at them when your real life has begun. You might be surprised by the similarities, and the differences.

It can be helpful to revisit this exercise, trying out another part of your new life. You may find that your image of yourself changes the more you consider it.

Constructing Your New Paper Identity

As you move into new consumer roles, be prepared to validate your paper identity. You may need your social security card to obtain a driver's license. You may need your passport to prove you are eligible to work in your new community. You may need your marriage license, divorce papers, and even death certificates of deceased family members.

As soon as you are committed to moving, begin to assemble these papers while you are still living in a place where you know your way around. Trying to locate a social security or passport office will add considerably to your stresses as a newcomer.

Boris learned a valuable lesson when he began putting his documents together for a move to Idaho. He had always believed he needed six credits to complete a bachelor's degree, but had put off completing the degree. Now, with two young children and a third on the way, he needed to qualify for a better-paying job. After much procrastination, Boris called the college registrar to learn how much work would be needed to complete his degree. To his amazement, Boris's college offered to give him six credits for his work experience with inner city teenagers. Boris moved to his new community armed with a new diploma, relieved he had not waited any longer.

══ Exercise ══
The Oracle

Write a series of predictions for the coming year:

- I think I'll look like . . .
- Here's how I've changed . . .
- What I hope will happen is . . .
- What I dread will happen is . . .

You can be funny, serious, melodramatic, factual—whatever works.

Anna, a marketing consultant, is moving to San Francisco from Arizona:

I will look paler but more stylish.

I'll have more cultural knowledge but my tennis game will be shot.

As I write, I look forward to the opera.

I dread finding a social life—I hear it's a tough city. I also dread the parking hassles, driving on those hills and being away from horseback riding.

Ricardo, a school counselor, is moving from Minneapolis to Miami:

A year from now, I'll be tanned and fit.

I'll drink less, eat more, and take more walks on the beach.

I'm looking forward to speaking Spanish. It's a second language down there.

I dread the heat of the summers and the humidity.

This exercise may seem simple, but the effects can be powerful, especially if you continue with this follow-up:

Test the Oracle

Hide your predictions in a safe place. You may want to hide them in a sealed envelope in a place where you can expect to run across it someday. For instance, if you move in summer, hide your notes with your income tax file. You'll come across it six or seven months later, long after you've forgotten what you've written.

You may be happier than you ever expected or you may be climbing the walls, ready to leave at a moment's notice. I guarantee there will be some surprises.

Hunting for a Home

Looking for a new home can be among the most stressful experiences you encounter. The home can be an important symbol of who you are. Hunting for a new home means looking for a place where your identity can put down new roots. "It's worse than being out of work," recalls Susan, who spent three weeks apartment hunting. "If you're out of work, you can stay home and deal with being out of work. If you're out of a home, you have nothing."

Consider the following options to help minimize your stress and help you stay on top of the situation.

Recognize the Local Housing Culture

Each region, sometimes each neighborhood, has its own housing culture. Culture includes language: "garden apartment," "hideaway apartment," "executive junior." You will have to research what each term means. In some parts of Canada, ordinary apartments are called "suites." As you study the want ads of your new city, you may find ads classified by neighborhoods you've never heard of: Sunset or Sunrise? Davie or Davidson? "Near Saint Joseph's school" means nothing to the newcomer, and just where is the "Art Museum Area?"

Even if you can identify the neighborhoods, you may be bewildered by the local style of giving directions. "Turn left where the old school used to be" means nothing to you. In Fort Lauderdale, people direct newcomers to the beach via Sunrise Highway, while all the overhead street signs say A1A or US 1.

Seek Small Doses of Control

Often you can gain control by investigating short-term alternatives. You will feel empowered if you can say, "If I don't feel comfortable with the options I see right away, I will be staying at the Hometown Arms for a month or two." Nearly all cities have month-to-month apartment options. Some hotels offer large discounts to long-term guests. Bill, who moves every two or three years, says, "I now look for the backup option before I look for a house or apartment. Before I talk to a real estate agent or a property manager, I have a list of short-term housing options."

Delay Long-Term Commitment

Be aware that your identity may change as you spend time in a new location. You may need time to find neighborhoods that express your identity. If a region is totally new to you, it might be wise to make moving a two-step process. Make a one-year commitment to a place that offers maximum efficiency and minimum paperwork. Use that year to learn about your options.

An experienced real estate agent in Fort Lauderdale says, "Most of my customers move down here thinking they know what they want. South Florida is different from just about any place in the United States. I urge them to wait for a year before they buy. You'd be amazed how many calls I get the following year, thanking me for discouraging them from buying right away. Now they know they want west side instead of east, or a condo instead of a house. They didn't know what they wanted till they lived here awhile."

Clare Cooper Marcus, a distinguished professor of architecture, has spent many years studying the psychological aspects of housing. In her book, *House as a Mirror of Self*, Marcus (1995, 223) writes that featureless, square, white-walled apartment buildings serve a special purpose as "transitional" housing. The bland white walls challenge you to impose your own design and personality. The sense of impermanence may actually be comforting. If you are undergoing many changes with this move, you may want to consider one of these square-box options for the short term.

Beware the Scarcity Trap

"Get 'em while they last" is a very effective sales pitch. You need to ask yourself, "Is this really all they have?" The answer is, "Probably not." The scarcity pressures can be more subtle. You may hear that it's "impossible to rent a place if you have a large dog" or that "Properties in that neighborhood are going quickly" or even that "You won't have much choice this time of year."

All of these statements may be true, but people have found wonderful places to live when the occupancy rate hovers at two percent, when they have three cats, and when they needed to move in twenty-four hours. A positive, determined attitude can offset a great deal of negative reality. You need to remember, however, that a positive attitude takes energy. If you are too exhausted to keep looking, stick with short-term alternatives: places you can tolerate for one month, six months, or a year.

Recognize Your Vulnerability

People who are overwhelmed by new situations can behave irrationally, even self-destructively. When you are new, you may be oblivious to important cues and you may therefore be tempted to seek help from anyone who crosses your path. You will be vulnerable to sales pitches from agents and advice from old-timers who claim to be experts. Some ways you can reduce your vulnerability include the following:

- *If at all possible, find your realtor while you remain in familiar surroundings.* Do your research from the comfort of home. You make better decisions when you are comfortable. Also, demand references from everyone who offers to represent you.

- *If you are totally new to an area, insist on using at least two different agents from two different companies.* "Yes, they all have the same listings," says Bernard. "However, they interpret those listings differently. Some are more willing than others to track down an elusive seller or landlord."

- *Ask to meet a few of your future neighbors.* It's a good sign if they talk to you first.

- *Talk to everybody you meet.* Even the people sitting next to you on the plane can be valuable sources of information. The odds are that half of the people on any flight live at either the origin or they live at the destination. If they're old-timers, they'll have additional insights into the housing culture.

- *Don't make decisions when you're exhausted.* Exhaustion causes confusion and slows down your thought processes. "I took a red-eye flight to begin my house-hunting trip," recalls Carla. "I flew from midnight to six A.M. through three time zones. As a result, I couldn't think clearly. I just wanted this trip to be over. Never again. Two days of alert activity are better than three half-dead ones."

- *Get advice from more than one source.* If you hear the same advice from three or four different sources, it's probably good advice.

Beware the Authority Trap

Moving company representatives, rental and real estate agents, lawyers, and other consultants will present themselves as experts. Most follow ethical guidelines, but don't assume that all have your best interest at heart. As one interviewee said, "When you're vulnerable, the sharks come after your blood."

To make yourself less vulnerable, consider the following steps:

- *Get references from everyone you deal with, especially if you are buying a home.* If you do not have time or energy to do this, or if you feel you do not trust the references, delay your commitment. By insisting on references, you establish yourself as a serious business person. Even if the resource was recommended by someone you trust, do your own investigating.

- *Know your rights and resources.* Nearly every community has a Real Estate Board that will discipline agents for unethical conduct. Bar associations have ethics committees. Moving companies are regulated by the Public Utilities Commission.

- *Remember that it's a business relationship.* They are your employees, not your friends. Even if an agent shows you around as a courtesy, he or she expects to be paid in referrals or future business.

- *Remind yourself to stay relaxed.* As you transact business and look for a new home, recite a protective mantra: "I do not need this person or this service. If they go away, I will find someone else. I am not in a hurry. I am not desperate. It is very unlikely that I, or my family, will sleep in the park. We do not have to settle for an intolerable solution."

Exercise
Visualize Your New Home

Whether buying or renting, try this exercise before you begin your search.

Plan fifteen to twenty minutes where you will not be interrupted.

Relax, close your eyes, get comfortable.

Ask yourself, what is my ideal home? Pay attention to any images that appear.

Where is the light? Do you see yourself at home in the evenings with a lamp? Or do you see sunny windows?

What is the shape of the rooms?

What is your view?

What kind of furniture do you see? Does it look like the furniture you have now?

Who do you see in the home with you? Are you entertaining friends, working in solitude in a study, relaxing with family?

Are you in a high-rise apartment building? Do you have a yard or garden?

Come out of the meditation slowly. Sit quietly for at least 30 seconds.

Write a summary of your vision. From these notes, write a visualization. Visualizations are written in the present tense. Do not force images. Sometimes people see a small movie screen in their minds, allowing the action to unfold as they watch. If you are uncomfortable with the image, stop. Perhaps this is the home you want to avoid.

If you can't visualize the entire home, visualize any small part. I found a great apartment once by visualizing wide windowsills where the cats could sprawl. I couldn't imagine anything else, but the apartment I found had windowsills and a lot more. Here are some examples:

I am now living in a beautiful high-rise apartment in a large city. Sunlight comes through the windows. The cats sprawl on the windowsills. I see plants hanging in the living room. There is a separate room for my home office, with a computer and separate phone line. The floors have warm brown carpeting. On the walls hang framed prints. I sip coffee as I type in the morning . . .

I am now living in a cozy three-bedroom home in a medium-sized city. The neighbors on the block are extremely friendly and the children play together after school. I see myself in the bright modern kitchen, baking cookies. The wood-paneled den holds our entertainment center and some comfortable chairs. Nobody minds if you put your feet on the furniture . . .

After you are comfortable visualizing your ideal home, talk to any family members or friends who may be sharing the home with you.

Return to your vision every day. Some people prefer to close their eyes and imagine themselves in the new setting. Others write out the dream, like set designers offering instructions to the carpenters.

It can also be helpful to try these visualizations with houses that you have looked at during your search. Visualize yourself living there. How does it feel? Is it easy to imagine? Does the house make you uncomfortable?

If you are ambivalent about a certain home, this visualization is a great way to find out what you really think.

═══ Exercise ═══════════════════════
Will I Be Happy Here?

This exercise will help you decide if you want to move into a specific place you are considering.

As you look at a potential house or apartment, ask yourself: Would my favorite objects fit nicely? Would my chairs and couch clash with the rug and the walls? Will my books fit?

If your possessions fit easily, you probably will too. The following are some good signs:

- You have lots of books and the dwelling comes with built-in bookshelves.

- You have two outdoor cats and the previous owner built a cat door.

- You can't tear yourself away from the view at one of the windows.

- At least one room has just the right amount of sun for your plant collection.

- There's a way to play your favorite music, loud, without disturbing the neighbors.

After you get settled, you will probably find at least half a dozen pleasant surprises in any new home, no matter how much you think you'll hate it.

"A great next-door neighbor."

"The best bakery in town, just down the street."

"Shelves built into the closet! I missed them when I looked at the apartment."

"A neighbor whose son became my son's best friend."

"The view from that window. I loved it."

"The garden just went wild in spring. I guess they planted a lot of perennials."

Take time to appreciate each discovery. Whether you hope to move in six months or wish you could stay forever, these discoveries will ease the stress of relocation.

Moving Tip

Make a List

The key to a move is planning. If you have sufficient advance notice, begin to organize your household six weeks ahead of time. Arrange to donate unwanted items as soon as possible so you'll have more space.

I definitely recommend making a checklist. You can purchase a book of checklists through your local or online bookstore. Here are some books that offer checklists: *Steiner's Complete How to Move Handbook* by Clyde Steiner (Dell, 1996); *Moving: A Complete Checklist and Guide for Relocation* by Karen G. Adams (Silvercat Publications, 1994); *Checklist for a Perfect Move* by Anne Colby (Main Street Book Editions, Doubleday, 1996). Your local bookstore or library may have others.

Your moving company will often include checklists in their booklets, or you can browse their websites to obtain a variety of useful ideas. Some of the recommendations may seem simplistic, but it's easy to take leave of your common sense amidst the frenzy of moving.

5

"Can't Turn Back Now!"

The Transformation Phase

Once you have left one home, bound for another, you exist in a temporary, in-between state: "you're neither here nor there." Georgianna, an elementary school teacher, summed it up nicely: "I don't think well till I feel settled. I'm not settled while I'm getting ready for a move and I'm not settled till—well, until I'm settled again. I can't concentrate. I'm supposed to be planning lessons and I'm way behind."

Your Identity in Transition

Trying to carry on with business as usual during a transformation can be exhausting and difficult. Historically, societies have developed rituals to protect new community members and keep them separate from those who are already settled. Those in the in-between state must accomplish special tasks to help them learn their new roles and statuses. They occupy special rooms or seats and wear distinctive clothing. Often their motivation is tested with fasting, sleep-deprivation, and various forms of "hazing."

When you move to a new community, you may feel as though you are undergoing similar ordeals. Your identity seems to shift, even disappear. Like those undergoing initiation rites, you lose your former identity but have not yet assimilated the new identity that you hope to achieve. Those already settled in the community may seem to be avoiding you.

Before you moved, you could express your self-concept by using and displaying your possessions and by engaging in activities you enjoy. You visited your favorite hangouts or cooked your favorite foods in a kitchen, and you knew where everything was. Your self-concept was reinforced and strengthened by your social identity as you interacted with people who knew you. Your paper identity smoothed many of your everyday activities.

Now your identity has begun to blur. Your possessions are locked in a moving van. You have access to only a small portion of your wardrobe and none of your furniture. When you arrive at your destination, your activities will be extremely limited and unfamiliar. You'll be surrounded by strangers. Your paper identity will need to be established to new businesses who have never seen you before and may act with suspicion or scrimp on service.

Once you have settled, you will begin building your new identity; but for now, your identity is changing so fast that you may feel anonymous and invisible, lost in transition, whether it lasts a few hours, days, or weeks.

Reframing Your Self-Concept

A great deal of your stress can be traced to the rapid changes in your self-concept. Losing touch with your identity can be a great source of anxiety. Though you might feel caught in a whirlwind, you can reframe your experience. Think of ways to describe this transition in a positive and creative way. This positive reframing helps you maintain a self-concept that will be strong enough to withstand change, yet flexible enough to learn a new life.

A Chance to Experiment with New Roles

You have fulfilled your obligations associated with previous roles and have not yet accepted new commitments. You can use this opportunity to evaluate the way you spend your time. You are free to design new roles, write a new script, and design a "new you" for your new life.

Jim was relieved to give up all his volunteer committee work. He used the transition time to plan more meaningful leisure activities in his new home. Marilyn decided to stop smoking when she moved. "I told everybody I was a non-smoker," she says, "so nobody offered me an ashtray and I was too embarrassed to change my mind."

A Time-out from a Busy Life

You can decide that, for the next few weeks, you are going to enjoy a break.

Hortense did not realize how much she was enjoying the in-between state until she got a call from the president of the board of a major charity in the new city. "Since I was taking a senior executive position, I was fairly high-profile," she says, "and there were stories about my promotion in the local papers. But I wasn't ready to make that commitment. I wanted to enjoy some time off and I didn't want to take time in the middle of this move to learn about the organization. I said, 'Call me after I've been on the job for a month. If you still want me, we'll talk.'"

Imagine that you're on vacation. Choose activities that you enjoy even though the setting will be unfamiliar. If your vacation typically includes visiting museums, a stop in an art museum will reinforce your self-concept, not to mention take your mind off the transition for a few hours.

"Driving across country was fun, once we got going," said Alison. "We knew we had nothing else to do. There was no point in rushing to get there, as our house wasn't ready. Camping out was something we had always done. Even in unfamiliar camp grounds, we felt at home."

Only a Few Days Out of My Whole Life

Transitions don't last forever: initiations are temporary and so is a move. A particularly useful technique involves reminding yourself that this event represents only a tiny slice of your life. Even boot camp comes to an end. You may feel overwhelmed, but this feeling won't last forever.

You can gain a sense of control by reminding yourself of the boundaries of this experience. How long will the experience last? "Two weeks," Marilyn told herself firmly. The moving company picked up her household on August 15. She knew she'd be in her new home by Labor Day at the latest, most likely with all her possessions surrounding her.

How intense can it be? "We won't starve. We'll be able to find vegetarian restaurants. We may have a few uncomfortable nights, but we will not have to sleep outdoors. We may be in a car ten hours a day, but we can take breaks and listen to our favorite music."

═══ **Exercise** ═══════════════════════════════
Face Your Fears

When you face what you dread the most, your fears lose power. Sometimes they disappear altogether.

Consider the following questions about your move:

- What do you dread most about moving?

- What do you enjoy most that you will be unable to do while you're in between two homes?

- How long will this in-between phase last?

For example:

I dread having to deal with the moving company. They're so arrogant. I hate arguing with people and they hold all the cards.

Between two homes, I can't just relax with a beer and a football game. I can't sit quietly and read a book with a cat in my lap. I can't eat a dinner I've cooked myself and linger over coffee with my family.

It will last two weeks. That's all! I may have to argue with the moving company when they load my stuff. That's half a day out of my life. I leave my present home on the tenth and my movers are due on the twenty-first. I won't be completely unpacked in three days, but I'll be able to sit in a chair and read a book. We can have dinner as a family the very first week.

When people discuss the traumas of moving, they rarely talk about those intense weeks during the actual move. They usually talk about settling into a new home, making friends, getting the kids into good schools. People get upset when the moving company breaks their favorite objects or when a shipment gets delayed. Yet six months later, these crises become interesting stories to share with other movers. Yours will, too.

"That Old Sweater Is Me, Too!"

During this transition, you are separated from your possessions. Watching your precious belongings disappear into a van can be scary. Most people admit they miss old friends, but some are embarrassed to admit they care for pets, furniture, or stereos. Comics like to joke about people who hang on to their favorite moth-eaten sweaters or that battered old sofa in the den. Yet, as we have seen, possessions contribute significantly to individual self-concept.

You have probably heard the term "comfort food," food that makes you feel safe, bringing back memories of security. People also have what might be called "comfort possessions." Almost any object can hold special meaning. Consumer researcher Russell Belk (1992) studied archives of Mormon missionaries who migrated to Utah under conditions of extreme hardship. Although their covered wagons were crowded, families went to great lengths to hold on to objects that held special meaning. People sat on rocking chairs atop their covered wagons; occasionally someone managed to move an entire piano.

═ **Exercise** ═══════════════════════
Fire Drill

What are your most cherished possessions? Which of your belongings holds special meaning for you?

One way to discover your priorities is to think of what you would do in the event of a fire. If you had only a few trips to carry belongings outside to safety, which items would you choose? What if you could only carry one armload? What would you grab?

As you work on your list, ask yourself how you will move these cherished objects to your new home. What can you keep with you during the trip? What will you pack with special care?

If it is at all possible, keep your most precious items with you—not in the moving van.

Many people find pets to be especially comforting. Of course, there are certain drawbacks during a long journey. You need to stop for water, make room in the car for food and pet carriers, and walk a dog or change a litter box en route. Your options for overnight motels will be limited. Cats like to hide just before you begin a day of driving. Yet even considering these difficulties, many people swear their furry companions helped them survive a move. I've heard dozens of variations of "Every night, no matter where I was, I took Fido for a walk and it felt just like home."

Opening the Closed Places

Perla Korosec-Serafty (1984) observes that houses have both secret and open places. Some places, notably attics and cellars, have the function of preserving objects and hiding them from public view. When you begin to move, you inevitably find yourself exploring the hidden places of your home. You probably have a kitchen drawer that hasn't been emptied in years. Packing up the attic or basement will force confrontation with a part of your identity that has not been visited for years.

Moving companies often quote a rate that includes packing. There are many economic advantages. The moving company accepts full responsibility for their own packing, and your prized glass table is more likely to arrive intact.

There are also psychological advantages to having the movers pack. Packers do not sort through your closets, sighing over the pants that won't fit anymore. Packers do not make judgments. An old chair? The big basket from the warehouse store? No problem. The battered scratching post so your cat will feel at home? A tag and some tape and it's loaded before you notice.

People often say, "I wish we had taken that lamp (or bookcase or chair) with us. I could really use it now." Unless you are on a really tight budget, err on the side of taking too much. You may decide to move that chair with the big hole or the threadbare sweater you haven't worn in years. And yes, when you get to your destination, you may decide that you need to donate a large box to the Salvation Army. This is a common experience among movers. Discarding unwanted items is just as easy *after* you have moved.

If you pack your own household, follow the example of the pros. Pack everything. Pack fast. And don't judge.

Transformation of Social Identity

"Being anonymous was the hardest part," said Jill, recalling a move to Chicago. "People would ask where I was moving to, and I'd have to explain that I was moving to Chicago. Then they would look at me with pity and say things about how people shoot each other on the streets and why am I doing that. Amazingly, after I moved, when I said I lived in Chicago, nobody messed with me. You don't criticize someone's hometown once they're there."

During the transition stage, many people feel like they have no control. Suddenly you depend on strangers—moving company sales reps, packers, car rental firms, real estate agents, property management companies—to them, you're nothing more than your paper identity. "I felt like everybody was trying to get a piece of what I had," Jill said. "Everybody wanted a piece of the action. Nobody cared if I got what I wanted. Nobody cared when my furniture arrived, as long as they didn't have to pay penalties. Nobody cared if we ended up with a broken-down hut in the worst neighborhood in town. As long as they got their money, they would tell me—and sell me—anything. I've never felt so alone."

"We're In This Together."

Initiation rituals typically force the initiates to pull together. Drill sergeants tell recruits in basic training, "Cooperate and graduate." Bonding is not accidental. Identity changes create loneliness. You have little in common with those who are left behind, but you are not yet accepted by your new community. Unlike Marine Corps recruits or sorority pledges, those who move have no cohort to share this adventure. You must create your own support system, by creating interactions with those who travel with you, or maintaining ties with those you leave behind.

If you move with a family, you will be around familiar people. But they may be stressed and irritable during relocation. Interactions that should be supportive often degenerate into irritated bickering. In order to foster cooperation, plan at least one enjoyable activity each day, where people can just enjoy each other's company. When driving across country, some families stop early to get in a swim at the motel pool. Build treats for the whole family into your schedule— pizza, a movie, a game, or sport.

As you plan your itinerary, schedule visits and phone calls with friends and relatives along the way. Remember your friend who retired to North Carolina? Why not stop in on your way from Florida to Washington? Take a few hours to share pizza and memories. Suddenly you're on familiar ground again: eating in a restaurant with someone you know, just the way you did back home.

Friends can also point out the positives that are easy for a frazzled mover to overlook. "Stopping to visit my friends Ricardo and Angela really helped," says Juanita, a human resource manager who drove from Kansas City to Boston. "They reminded me I was undertaking a major project and they were impressed when I kept going through a thunderstorm. They told me I'd be speaking Spanish with a Boston Irish accent. That night was the highlight of my trip."

Even the most trivial compliment can seem welcome, say experienced movers. You feel good when you hear, "Wow! You got all that stuff into this little car!" or, "Your kids are doing great. Mine never sit still for so long."

The Paper Transformation

Suddenly your wallet doesn't look the same: a new driver's license, new library card, new health insurance ID, and new membership cards. You may have even replaced your credit cards to develop a relationship with your new bank or earn frequent flyer miles on the only airline that serves this region. Each new piece of paper says something about who you are in your new location.

When you move, your paper identity becomes subject to scrutiny. Whether you rent or buy a new home, your credit will be checked. Some people feel exposed and vulnerable when they have to prove themselves all over again. For George, replacing a lost social security card was the last straw: "I've been working for thirty years. Each year I pay into social security. And I've been driving for thirty years with a perfect record. I know my number. Now these idiots want to see an actual social security card—that blue and white thing—so I can get a new driver's license."

Those who move abroad may have to endure background checks and unwanted medical exams. Customs officials sometimes ask you to list everything you are bringing into the country, item by item. "I felt invaded," recalls Eve, who moved to Canada and then moved back. "It was like an initiation rite. We filled out all these forms and I bet nobody even looked at them."

=== Exercise ===
The Energy Map

During a move, it is easy to get caught up in frustrations, losing your sense of identity. This exercise helps you design an Energy Map—a plan to help you make the best use of your energy resources on your journey. You can use it whether you fly, drive, or take a boat to your new destination.

Identify some activities you enjoy (with your family or by yourself if you're traveling alone).

Examples:

Eating out
Taking the family for a picnic
Going for a swim
Watching a movie

Draw a timeline of your journey, from the time you leave one home to the time you arrive at the next, in two-hour time blocks. If you are traveling a longer distance, or going overseas, you may wish to use longer time chunks.

Note which time periods represent the greatest energy drains.

Packing the night before
Loading the car
Stuffing the cats into their carriers
Fighting traffic on the freeway

Following periods of energy drain, schedule an Energy Boost, an activity that represents something you like to do. Schedule something at least every four hours, even if you only have time for a small treat. If you are driving, be aware that more than eight hours a day on the road can exhaust even professional drivers. Have you ever been so tired that you took the wrong exit and lost an hour getting back? That episode might have been prevented by a half-hour energy boost—a much more pleasant way to spend the time.

Here are some examples of what your Energy Map will look like.

Ralph's Energy Map:

6:00 A.M.:—Home. Load car, walk dog, put family in car.

8:00 A.M.:—On road. Sit in traffic. Energy drain.

10:00 A.M.:—ENERGY BOOST: Stop at park. Take twenty minutes to stretch, walk dog, be silent. Give everyone alone time.

10:30 P.M.:—Another two hours of driving. Energy Drain.

12:30 P.M.:—ENERGY BOOST: Picnic.

2:00 P.M.:—Difficult stretch of mountain driving. Big Drain.

4:00 P.M.:—Arrive at motel. Into swimming pool! ENERGY BOOST.

Karen's Energy Map:

5:30 A.M.:—Stuff cat into carrier and get cab to airport.

7:30 A.M.:—On plane, cramped and miserable. Cat vanishes into baggage compartment. MAJOR ENERGY DRAIN.

11:30 A.M.:—Land in new city. Find cab that will take cat and self to new apartment. VERY MAJOR ENERGY DRAIN.

3:00 P.M.:—Appointment for massage and facial (arranged ahead of time, by phone).

7:00 P.M.:—Take myself out to elegant restaurant for salad and glass of wine.

9:30 P.M.:—Bubble bath. A long phone call to my favorite person in the world.

For six hours, Karen has given up nearly all activities and possessions that express her identity. She's a number on a ticket stuffed into an airplane seat. Therefore, she plans a series of major Energy Boosts for the end of her day.

"Everything That Could Go Wrong Has Gone Wrong."

Although nearly every move offers a few hair-raising episodes, some people do experience one disaster after another. Martha says she is one of the luckiest or unluckiest movers in the world, depending on your viewpoint. Eight years later, she talks as if she moved yesterday: "I was so excited about my move to Chicago from Baltimore! I had a new job, a company car, and a big promotion to senior management. My friends held farewell parties. The company bought my house. Everything was set.

"And then my company car was stolen. My purse, with my wallet and keys, were inside the car. It was a total catastrophe. The moving company was scheduled to pick up my furniture the very next day, but the car had to be loaded first, so they just waited around while the police looked for my car. We finally found the car vandalized beyond repair. I had to find a place to stay for a few days while we sorted things out. My friends kept saying, 'Why are you here? We just had your party!' When I finally got to Chicago, I had to arrange for a new company car. I was exhausted for weeks. What a way to begin a new job."

When you find yourself putting out one fire after another, you may have the natural urge to keep pressing ahead. "No time to stop," you mutter, as you grit your teeth and carry on. Yet if you find yourself running into walls, the best thing to do is to stop running. Take an afternoon off. Go to an art museum, a ball game, or a movie—an activity that will distract you for a few hours. Work out in the gym or go for a run.

A Time-out Is Not Frivolous

You need to understand why you are experiencing chaos. You may start to think it's fate: you just weren't intended to move anyway. However, you may want to consider other explanations.

You're so tired you can't function anymore. Moving is exhausting. If you're packing up kids, pets, and possessions, you're performing in real physical labor. The process of making arrangements will pull you in several directions at once, each one unfamiliar, possibly irritating, and sometimes even scary.

When your tired, you make mistakes. Then you have to spend more energy undoing your mistakes. The only cure is to stop and rest. You might be surprised when you come home after a relaxing run and find a problem-solving message on the answering machine.

You are resisting this move. If you feel you have no choice and that you must leave a place you love, you may find yourself acting with less than your usual care.

"I didn't proofread our house for sale ad, and I wondered why nobody called. They printed our number wrong."

"I forgot to tell the moving company not to come on Tuesday. Nobody was home when they came to give us our estimate. It took two weeks to reschedule and they became increasingly difficult to work with."

"I am usually so careful about confirming everything and taking numbers. And I just let things slide. I guess I hoped the move would just go away."

You need energy to cope with the situation you are leaving. You may be moving away from a difficult situation: a city you hate, an abusive job, a painful divorce. If you are still dealing with your emotions regarding these situations, you will be using energy that could otherwise be used to help you move.

You don't know the rules. You may be moving to a community so different from your own that you feel you need an interpreter to survive. "Where I come from, realtors help people with rentals as a goodwill gesture. When I asked for this service, the agent just gave me a sales pitch on why we should buy right away."

The clock is ticking. You may be pressed for time because your employer wants you to report for work at once. Time pressure can distort your thinking, leading to careless mistakes and bad decisions.

Sometimes the most important step in overcoming these situations is, simply, recognition. Once you become aware of what is going on you may find that the pressure eases. If you're so stressed that you cannot function on the job, or if your emotions are causing distress to friends and family members, you may want to seek professional assistance.

If you are becoming accident-prone, do not wait. A relocation presents numerous opportunities for accidents even when you're upbeat and positive. Seek help at once, even if you must move early or delay your departure in order to get access to resources.

"This Isn't Me!"

Eleanor and Jack rented a small tract house while their future home was undergoing renovations. "I almost cried every time I saw that ugly wallpaper," Eleanor remembers. "There were cracks in the walls and the floors were disgusting. Everything about that horrid little house cried, 'Junk!'"

You can feel out of place even if the house you buy or rent is well-maintained and aesthetically pleasing. Anne rented a charming condominium that her landlords, a retired couple, had purchased as investment property. The owners had lavished loving concern on the decorations, choosing wallpaper, lighting, and appliances that displayed their exquisite taste. They wanted tenants who would appreciate what they had done and they looked over Anne's furniture with a critical eye. Anne always felt her landlords were looking over her shoulder. "I knew that, legally, they had no right to comment on my furniture or the pictures on my walls," Anne said. "But I was living their dream, not mine. There was no way I could create a home that was me."

Anne stayed two years, then moved into a rental-only building with the usual white walls, mini-blinds, and neutral carpets. "I could change the whole look of a room just by adding pictures and moving furniture around," she realized. "Nobody cared what I did as long as I paid the rent on time. It wasn't very homey, but I slept better at night."

Moving Tip

Rental Wanted

If you are seeking an unusual rental situation, consider running a "Rental Wanted" advertisement yourself. Learn how to place a want ad by surfing the newspaper's website or checking the local classified section. Most newspapers accept credit cards so you can place your ad before you've left home. Emphasize that you are a great tenant seeking a great landlord. Some people worry about having their answering machines filled with bizarre messages, but in my experience the replies are few and serious.

6

"I've Moved—but Nobody Else Can Tell the Difference!"

The Integration Phase (The First Six Months)

Now that you have unpacked, you are ready to begin your new life. Moving yourself and your possessions transforms you into a new resident, but integrating into your new community may take some time.

The Smooth Start

Some people feel at home immediately. They may owe their good fortune to detailed planning and preparation, or they might be just plain lucky. Here are a few reasons for a smooth transition.

Your new identity may feel like a continuation, not an interruption. "I felt at home right away," said Henry, who moved to New York as a young artist. "For the first time in my life, I felt surrounded by people like me." For Georgianna, "Moving to Ohio from Nevada was a homecoming. I'm a Midwesterner by birth and it's in my blood."

You may find an instant social circle. Allen and his wife found the same church structure all over the world. Ron, a skilled Morris dancer, was welcomed into a local group that needed experienced performers. Mary, a lifelong bird-watcher, attended a meeting of the local Audobon society, and within months she was elected treasurer.

Your job may create a social identity. Marina, moving to a small college town, said, "We were accepted right away by Justin's colleagues. The faculty and staff do a lot of social things together. They're really neat people.

The Stressful Start

Most people have a harder time settling in. Here are a few reasons for a bumpy transition.

You're just tired. During the first frantic weeks, many newcomers are so exhausted from moving that they forget all their usual coping mechanisms. They say things like, "My circuits overloaded," or, "I just shut down." Fatigue and loneliness can distort your perceptions and feelings, making a difficult situation seem unbearable.

"After thirty days," Annette says frankly, "I was ready to throw in the towel. I wanted to give up my job, sell the house at a huge loss, and move back home." Fortunately, Annette's accountant convinced her to wait awhile, and she now looks back at this period as the "darkness before the dawn."

It seems to go on forever. Most researchers and counselors agree: People need a minimum of two years to make new friends and develop meaningful ties to a new location, regardless of culture, age group, and lifestyle.

You're still learning the culture. "Around here, you get a smile and a hug even if we hate your guts," says Shelley, whose soft Southern accent belies her cynicism. "Up in New York, you get a snarl even if they're your best friend. Go figure."

Homesickness and Isolation

After you move, you may encounter the two biggest obstacles that surface during the first six months: homesickness and isolation. Each feeds off the other. As you grieve for the life you left behind, it becomes hard to connect to the new life around you. At the same time, when you have a difficult time connecting to your new location, you will romanticize the connections you left behind.

As you begin to feel more comfortable with your new identity, these feelings will slowly melt away. As you strengthen your self-concept, you begin to feel stronger, even when you know few people in the new community. By connecting with yourself, you will take the first steps toward connecting with others.

"I'm Not Supposed to Be Homesick—but I Am!"

People often feel embarrassed to admit they miss their former residence, yet nearly everyone does. Even very small losses trigger homesickness. Years after emigrating to the west, refugees from war-torn countries will still miss certain foods they grew up with.

You may also find yourself mourning your former competence, the sense that you can handle whatever problems come your way. Before you moved, you knew who to call for help when something broke or someone got sick. Now you face dilemmas that seem new, even bizarre: "The landlord complained we used too much water"; or "It was three o'clock in the morning when the dishwasher flooded"; or "My cat decided to stop eating the day after I moved in."

Before you moved, you could call for help and a familiar voice would answer. Now you have to figure out which number to dial, and when you call, you will be negotiating with a stranger.

Homesickness can be viewed as a type of grief. Homesick people often feel depressed, anxious, and even absent-minded. During your first six months in a new location, you may find yourself locking your keys in the car, forgetting a pot on the stove till it boils over, or misplacing your credit cards. Frustrating, yes, but very common.

"Nobody Understands."

When you call close friends and family, you may encounter new challenges to your social identity: they can't understand why you're having problems. You can expect serious expressions of disbelief if you're unhappy after a move to a prized location: fabled San Francisco, fast-growing Atlanta, a picturesque village in Vermont, or a tourist destination in Florida. "How can you hate San Francisco?" Julie's brother asked in bewilderment. "I went to two conventions there and I wanted to stay forever." Julie was learning to park on steep hills, wake up in fog, and find her way around a city where she knew no one outside her job. The moving company charged an extra three hundred dollars to move her furniture into her quaint little apartment, which featured steep stairs and no elevators. Julie suspected she might learn to love the city, but for now she'd just as soon be back in Delaware. But to her brother, she was in paradise.

Learning a New Language

When you move, even if you don't leave the country, you have to learn a new language. Alaskans will call you a "cheechako" (newcomer), advise you to buy big white "bunny boots," and recall the last time they "went outside" (left Alaska, usually to visit the "lower 48"). You may put "tags" on your car instead of license plates. And when a Canadian promises to send something "by courier," wait for the overnight express van.

Even when you use the same words, you may not be communicating. "I felt that everything I said came out wrong," said Sally, after moving from Boston to Atlanta. She may be right. Deborah Tannen (1986) notes that regional speech patterns create interpersonal conflict. New Yorkers, as well as others from East Coast urban areas, tend to interrupt others during conversation, rather than wait for pauses. They also do not pause to allow others to speak. The New Yorker who follows her normal speech patterns will seem rude and pushy when she moves south.

"People I Want to Meet Are Too Busy for Me."

Tina moves every few years for her husband's corporation. Because she's always a newcomer, she rarely gets asked to assume leadership roles in community activities, and her job prospects are limited. She's been studying for an MBA: "It's like that paradox where the closer you get, the farther away the finish line seems. Every school has different course requirements. I'm always starting over."

Her neighbor Nancy, after ten years in the community, is a parent, wife, and sister-in-law who entertains her husband's relatives at Christmas. She is also a bank teller, PTA committee member, church member . . . and the list goes on.

As you develop your social identity, you become involved in more activities. You join clubs and get elected to office and soon every minute has been booked. When your mother-in-law shows up, you're on overload. And that is why Nancy, a truly caring person who'd love to make some new friends, probably won't become friends with Tina. There just aren't enough hours in her day.

As a result, newcomers often find themselves meeting people with a lot of time on their hands. Pauline, who loves BBC television, remembers the line in *Brideshead Revisited* about spending your second year getting rid of the friends you made in the first year. "It happens over and over," she says. "I thought I was making a friend at my alumni club when a woman called and invited me to lunch. After a couple of meetings, I realized she was desperately lonely and she had some serious problems with social skills. She kept asking me personal questions and bringing me little gifts. I realize now why she glommed on to the new woman in town. Busy people just take longer to get to know." The dandelion is the first flower to appear in the spring. The roses come much later, but they're well worth the wait.

"I Feel Like I'm an Alien from Another Planet."

Marvin, newly graduated from college, rented a charming in-law apartment in San Francisco. He was thrilled to get a bargain: a management trainee's salary didn't go far in those days. "It was just like *Seinfeld*," he recalls. "Everybody used my apartment as their apartment. Neighbors would walk in without knocking and they got upset if I locked the door. The worst thing was my landlady. She'd sit in my living room and smoke while I was out. I'd come in and smell smoke. Finally I just gave up and moved to a regular boxy apartment with a real landlord and a deadbolt lock. It was just too weird."

Looking back, Marvin realizes he just didn't know how to read the situation. "Someone who knew the city would have smelled a rat. The worst part was that I had nobody to ask. I didn't know a lawyer or even any friends who knew the local real estate situation. I thought, 'Hey, this is San Francisco. Maybe they're all like that!'"

Curing Homesickness

Here are some remedies that can help treat your homesickness. You can try any combination that appeals to you.

Put Together an Emotional First Aid Kit

When you go on vacation, you pack sunblock, Band-Aids, and insect repellent, as well as basic medications for possible encounters with local food and water. To counter your feelings of homesickness and isolation, prepare an emotional first aid kit: a collection of methods that help you cope with the stress you are likely to encounter. You might include some of the following items:

- Your coping phrases from Chapter 4, perhaps modified for longer-term stress situations

- Meditation and visualization tapes

- A book or a tape of yoga exercises

- Phone numbers of friends and family who can be called if you really need to talk. You might divide your friends into categories: someone to laugh with; someone who will listen; someone who just moved a year ago and can offer good advice.

- Music that relaxes you

- Photos that make you happy

Plan Rituals to Help You Feel More Settled

Honor your new home. An expert in the psychology of consumers Russell Belk (1988) notes that people often hold rituals to transform a house or apartment into an extension of themselves. Some people connect to their new homes by giving it a thorough cleaning. Others break in their new homes by hosting a party or hanging a favorite painting on the wall.

Carlos's job as a geologist requires him to relocate frequently, so he has developed a ritual for moving in. He unpacks his stereo system first, so he can finish unpacking while listening to his favorite music. This ritual allows him to combine what is new and strange with what is familiar. "The music seems to seep into the walls," he says. "It transforms the house and makes it mine."

Celebrate everyday life. In an exercise in chapter 1 you were asked to recount some of your daily rituals. You've left many of these rituals behind. Now you can create new rituals as you develop the routines that make you feel at home.

Jan reluctantly moved with her husband to a new city. When she arrived she felt particularly isolated during the day. While she searched for a job, she would start her day at a coffee shop in a nearby mall. She began to look forward to this morning ritual and the routine gave her a sense of taking charge.

Liven Up Your Holidays. Holidays offer special opportunities to create your own rituals. You may decide to alter traditional rituals to take advantage of local opportunities. Spending their first Christmas away from home in San Francisco, one young couple decided to leave behind the traditional turkey-with-family ritual. They arranged a party for their new friends, featuring Chinese and Japanese cuisine, foods that were not available in their former hometowns.

Keep Yourself Busy

Institutions that have to deal with large numbers of new people have fine-tuned this principle. Whether attending boot camp or boarding school, newcomers find their first days are so full that there is no time to be homesick.

You can be your own headmaster or drill sergeant and devise a schedule. You need variety as well as routine. A trip to the mall is a good way to get out of the house—but not five days a week. Reading and watching TV do not count! You need to be active. If your budget permits, attend a movie, play, or concert. If you want to design a quiet evening at home, take a few minutes to go for a walk, browse through a bookstore, and perhaps rent a video before collapsing on the couch.

Choose activities to nurture yourself, not to meet people. Donna attended a church in her neighborhood because her new neighbors told her it was a good place to meet people, but she had never been religious and found that she did not feel comfortable attending services. John was encouraged to join a wine-tasting club for single people over thirty, but he found that he had little in common with the members.

Self-nurturing is especially important for the newcomer. When you take care of yourself, you communicate strength and confidence to others. If you are seen as vulnerable and needy, you will attract negative people and negative experiences.

"I attended a woodworking class because I like to work with my hands," said Michael. "Since I didn't know anybody, I had time to try something I'd always wanted to do. I didn't care about meeting new people and at first I thought I wouldn't. After a few months of carving, I signed up for an advanced section. People complimented the work I was doing and eventually some of them began to talk to me. One of the guys invited me to a party at his house and I met a lot of people."

The chart you made in the "What's the Difference" exercise in chapter 3 can help you stay on track. You may have forgotten that you promised yourself you'd get a dog or take opera lessons. Do not wait till you "feel more settled." When you feel more settled, you'll have even less time and energy. You need to move now.

One word of caution: Avoid making long-term social commitments until you have an opportunity to learn what you're getting into. The goal is growth and fulfillment, not keeping busy. If you join a club or a volunteer group, you may discover you've made a mistake. You may create bad feelings if you try to resign.

Animal rescue organizations urge people to wait until they're settled to adopt a pet. Usually that is good advice. Animals will feel your stress and add to your workload. Adoption of a pet should be viewed as a lifetime commitment. On the other hand, I know people who adopted a full-grown dog or cat within days after moving to a new house or apartment. They had wanted a pet long before the move and they understood what was involved. I once adopted a four-year-old cat three days after moving to a new city. I left both job and city within six months, but the cat stayed with me for eleven years.

Get Out and Explore!

Being unable to find your way around can make you feel helpless. Four months after moving to a Midwestern city, Bonnie said, "The only thing that still makes me feel new is not knowing the road names. I still get confused about which way is north, south, east, and west." John added, "I still feel like a stranger when I'm with my new friends. They discuss places they have visited. I'm forever asking, 'Where is that?'"

═══ Exercise ═══
Exploration Game

Pick a type of retail store where you like to shop. Do you like bakeries? bookstores? toy stores? health food stores? Find three or four of these stores in the phone book.

If you don't want to be tempted to spend money, you can also explore parks, zoos, museums, or branches of your public library. Find their locations on a map and visit. Become a tourist for a day.

Many cities offer guided tours by buses, ferry boats, or trolleys. These tours offer a fast way to learn the city's history and to gain an appreciation for your city's attractions. Along the way, you will learn new roads and neighborhoods. You will find some stores that will become permanent fixtures in your new life. You may find yourself on a street where you feel so uncomfortable you won't get out of the car.

If friends or family members go along for the ride, ask them to call out street names as you drive. Next time someone refers to "Iris Drive" or "Kendalwood Circle," you will have a visual memory to connect with the name.

Journal Your Progress

Even though you feel homesick and tense on a day-to-day basis, you're probably making progress. Sometimes the changes are so minor you don't notice them. A journal is a great way to make yourself aware of the progress you are making.

Exercise
My Journal

Start a journal. Spend a few minutes every day writing down your thoughts and feelings. Here are some questions to answer in your journal?

• What felt new and unfamiliar today?

The new house felt cold. It wasn't really cold. We had plenty of heat. It just felt that way when we moved in.

• How do I feel about what is new? Am I eager to learn more?

• Did anything remind me of where I lived before?

I walked down a new street and suddenly, just across the way, was a row of old houses that reminded me of my childhood in Europe. I was taken back to the sounds and smells of twenty years ago. It was very comforting.

• What would I like to change in the present?

• What happened today that made me feel more at home here?

I called a cab to go to the airport. I gave them directions for a short cut to my house. They knew exactly what I was talking about.

- What was especially irritating or upsetting?

  These people in Connecticut do not know how to drive. They don't signal for lane changes. They stop and go. Back in California, they'd all get tickets.

  When you review your pages, notice how you have changed.

- What irritated you three months ago? Do you still get irritated by the same things? Has anything changed in your environment?

  Amazing. I just had a business trip to California. They drive a lot worse than I remember. I forgot how they tailgate out there— bumper-to-bumper at eighty miles an hour. I was glad I didn't have to face that every day.

Savor Your Small Moments of Pleasure

When you are extremely stressed, you may get caught up in frantic activity, focusing only on the negatives that arise. It can be difficult to stop the cycle, yet even fifteen minutes of relaxation or fun can send you back refreshed and ready to tackle the rest of your day. Think of some time-outs you enjoy. Here are a few to get you started.

- Sharing a glass of wine with your significant other
- Swimming at the pool or a walk along the lake
- Listening to a favorite piece of music
- Reading a best-selling thriller
- Having coffee or lunch at a fun restaurant
- Attending a movie or concert
- Visiting an art museum

There are no rules—except that you do only what you like, not what you think you should enjoy. And most important, acknowledge that you had fun and that it felt good.

Build a Six-Month Identity

Many people find themselves doing things during the first few months that they have never done before or since. By way of analogy, ocean liners are built to cruise smoothly over long stretches without interruption, but they need to be towed out to sea by a small tugboat. Consider your first six months as a tugboat guiding you safely past unfamiliar narrow passageways. Once safely at sea, you can release the tugboat with relief and gratitude. Here are some activities that can smooth the transition:

Sandra, was newly divorced when she relocated. She went to the movies three times a week for her first month. "My apartment was half-furnished and I didn't know anybody. Right after the divorce, I was advised to do things on my own, even if it felt uncomfortable. Moving is like divorce, I figured, and the only thing I could find was the local movie house."

Looking back, Sandra says, "I could have done worse. It got me out of the house. I got to know the neighborhood as I drove back and forth. Eventually I started taking little detours." Sandra got an unexpected benefit: she discovered she really liked film and wanted to learn more about it. As the new school year began, she picked up a booklet for a community college, enrolled in a film criticism course, and began to study film-making.

Develop Your Creativity

Psychologist Kurt Lewin developed a theory of change that has been applied extensively in the business world. People tend to become frozen in familiar patterns. In order to change, they need to thaw out before they can freeze into a new routine. By loosening you up, creativity can help you deal with change at all levels.

Plan a major creative effort for your first six months. Tim joined a sculpting class for the first and last time in his life. "I didn't meet anyone in the class. And no, I didn't find a new creative outlet or a lifetime hobby. I just wanted to stay busy and get out of this apartment. And I wanted something to think about besides work."

Is there a creative activity you've always wanted to try? Janet had always wanted to play the piano, but she held herself back: "It costs money and, anyway, how can I practice when I live in an apartment?" Music lessons have changed since Janet's childhood. The local university offered music classes and practice rooms with pianos, and she could buy an electronic keyboard with earphones for less than the cost of a pair of new shoes.

Take a class in an artistic medium that interests you: painting, creative writing, ceramics, flower arranging, quilting, glasswork, or woodwork. If you already have training, you may be able to obtain studio space, but many people find it is cost effective to take a class just to obtain space. Creativity thrives on interaction with others and you may enhance your skills more than you expected.

Get Physical

Don't be surprised if you feel relief from most symptoms of homesickness after a run, a long walk, a racquetball game, or an aerobics class. Like creative effort, physical activity also creates a new, stronger identity. A ten-session class in weight-training became a lifetime fitness style for Glenda, who got a kick out of "pumping iron" with the guys in the gym. Larry, a newly divorced security guard, discovered he could meet women and get a great workout by taking aerobics.

Build an Escape Hatch

As you begin to build your identity from the inside out, don't be surprised to feel busier and happier. At the same time, don't head for deep water: you are building a tugboat, not an ocean liner. A good rule of thumb is, "Don't sign up for anything unless you are willing to forego the fee if it turns out you've made a mistake."

Most creativity classes will be fun and supportive, but you may get a dud. I once signed up for a drawing class that was crowded and disorganized. Although the class was billed as an amateur class to develop creativity, the instructor became irritated with people who didn't catch on fast enough. The class had become a source of irritation, not fun. Frustration is not a helpful way to cope with stress.

How NOT to Deal with Homesickness

When people feel stressed and pressured, they tend to fall into comfortable patterns of behavior that have worked for them in the past. What's easy is often not what's best. In a new environment, these patterns can actually be destructive. Here are two tempting traps you probably want to avoid.

The Shopping Trap

Unhappy newcomers often seek relief at the nearby mall. "I've been very unhappy," wrote Helena, a full-time mother of two, who found herself living in a California suburb following her husband's transfer. "I keep buying things for me, things for the house, for the kids. I've never done this before, but I keep doing it."

Shopping can help people feel better. After all, it's something you know how to do. You feel comfortable with the sales clerks. You're in control and the transactions move at your own pace. A day at the mall can remind you of "The Real Me." Unfortunately, that feeling is often short-lived. Many newcomers find themselves buying all sorts of things they don't need. Now they have two problems: they're unhappy *and* they're in debt.

If you want to treat yourself, seek refuge in activity. Arrange for a massage or a facial. Join a health club. Take yourself out to lunch at a new restaurant. The benefits of these experiences will last longer than buying something that ends up in the closet because it reminds you of an unhappy time in your life.

The Confidante Trap

Psychologist Shirley Fisher (1989) warns against confiding too easily in others. When you are new to a location, it can be tempting to share your frustrations with colleagues from work, with neighbors, or with people you meet at the gym or the golf course. While nearly everyone gives in to this temptation at some point during a move, you have to remind yourself that you are dealing with people who, after all, are still strangers.

As a new member of the community, you do not know all the connections and you may need years to learn. "I was so embarrassed," says Thea, two years after she'd moved to Sacramento, California. "I signed up to volunteer as a counselor at a women's center. I confided to one of the women that I really, really hated my job. I talked about my horrible boss. And yes, it was just like a bad movie: she was best friends with my boss's wife. I un-volunteered real fast."

When people ask how you like your new home, most of the time they want to hear that you are happy. After all, they're probably happy here or they'd have left long ago. Long-term residents rarely realize how tightly they've woven their own networks and how difficult it is for you to fit in. Kevin tried to get a recommendation to a pediatrician for his young son who suffered from severe asthma. Prominent businesspeople were happy to refer him to their own physicians. "What they didn't know," Kevin said, "was that all these doctors had closed practices and were no longer taking new patients. We had to drive our son fifty miles to find a specialist we felt we could trust."

Even if the old-timers secretly hate your new city, they will probably resent hearing these complaints from a newcomer. It's the same principle as criticizing a member of the family: "I can say it because I'm one of them, but you can't." Alternatively, they may feel trapped themselves. Your ability to move away can be quite threatening to them.

Should You Get Professional Help?

Many newcomers consider this option during the first bout of homesickness. Definitely seek help immediately

- if you are seriously depressed, *especially if you have any suicidal thoughts*

- if you are unable to function at work

- if you find yourself experiencing sudden changes in the way you relate to your family, *especially if you become enraged at your children for small offenses*

- if you find yourself having a series of accidents, whether those accidents occur in the car, the home, or elsewhere

- if you are also experiencing severe stress from another life transition, such as divorce, sudden unemployment, or the death of a spouse

- if you experience physical symptoms of stress, such as insomnia or severe stomach ailments, *especially if you have never had those symptoms before*

There are other more subtle reasons for seeking professional help after a move.

You may find that all sorts of issues bubble into your consciousness. You may begin recalling memories from childhood or conflicts from college that you haven't remembered for years. You may experience sudden insights or turmoil as you reflect on issues that seem completely unrelated to the move.

You may need a safe place to share your feelings. "I was desperately lonely," recalls Karen, "and I found myself spilling my guts at my workplace. I told the therapist I just needed a safe place to share. I began to remember an abusive relationship from my sophomore year in college—something I thought I'd resolved. And that reminded me of my brother who died when I was in high school. And then . . . well, I needed to talk."

You may just need someone to talk to. Nancy, whose consulting firm assigned her to a small mining town, decided to use her company's mental health benefits so she could talk to someone: "I was the only professional woman in town and I was really isolated." She admits that "this worked only because it was very, very short-term. The therapist himself warned me that therapy is no substitute for friendship."

Choosing a therapist can be difficult in a new environment. You may not feel sufficiently comfortable asking strangers for a referral. "I had to call four people before I found a counselor I liked," says Philip, a technical trainer who had grown up in the South Bronx and who had reluctantly accepted a transfer to Omaha. "Three of them said they'd never met anyone like me before and I think they were put off by my accent. Maybe it's just my imagination, but I was very glad to find a guy who'd studied in New York. He understood why I missed the old neighborhood."

Be very clear on what you expect from a professional. It's not enough to say, "I've moved!"

You may want to learn the therapist's views about relocation, making sure he or she understands the stresses involved in relocation. You may want to look for a therapist who is familiar with places where you have lived, or people from those places. Another option is to establish a telephone relationship with a therapist from your former home.

Since you don't know people's connections yet, you may want to investigate possible conflicts of interest. Marianne felt a warm rapport with her therapist, Juanita. However, after several months of satisfying work, Marianne began dating Bob, who coached basketball at the local high school. One day Marianne said, "Bob and I might move away together. He really hates his job, especially with that new principal they got. That guy sounds like a real SOB . . . " There was an unusual silence from Juanita. Then, "We may have to stop therapy," she said. "I'm the principal's wife. I just kept my own name professionally."

"Is It Okay That I'm Happy Here?"

Roy Baumeister (1986), a psychologist who writes about identity issues, found that people sometimes felt they were betraying their former community by adapting too well to their new location. You have gotten so caught up in your new life that you have little in common with your old friends. You may write fewer letters. The telephone dates you arranged so carefully seem to disrupt your schedule. Recognizing that you are no longer close with these old friends can be a lonely feeling.

Grief May Be Delayed

Suzanne was delighted when her husband's company assigned him to Santa Barbara. She would be near her newly married daughter and her newly retired brother. The movers arrived on time and delivered their household goods intact. She had no trouble finding a job as an accounting assistant and her husband's promotion allowed them to live comfortably.

Six weeks after she had moved, Suzanne woke up thinking, "Something is wrong here." She had trouble describing the feeling. She wasn't unhappy, yet she missed her old home in one of Philadelphia's suburbs. She missed the cold weather in September. Her new job turned out to be a step down. She tried to tell herself, "You're just imagining things. We'll be fine here." Yet the feeling wouldn't go away.

Suzanne was probably having a delayed grief reaction. She had not mourned the loss of her former residence, which she felt acutely each day. She had not acknowledged her own sadness and her deep love for the Pennsylvania countryside. Before she could move on, she had to grieve what she had left behind.

Surprises Happen

Even a successful, happy move can encounter turbulence along the way. Nearly everyone reports a surprise after a year, even after eighteen months: "Things are not what I expected." The surprise may be small: you can't find a health club or a restaurant that serves your favorite kind of food. Sometimes the surprise is large and shocking: a child's school system seems deficient, the neighbors who seemed friendly turn out to be prejudiced and hostile, you get robbed and the police don't seem to care.

A New Multicultural Identity

By moving, you have gained exposure to different cultures or subcultures. You have had opportunities to gain fresh insights and understanding. "After I moved to a small town in Michigan," Sally said, "I kept in touch with friends from Boston. They reminded me there were other worlds: art galleries, traffic, underground subway systems, and snow. I wanted to keep the feeling that I had a foot in each world."

Moving Tip

Shipping Your Pets

Your veterinarian can advise you about shipping pets. Dogs do well in cars, but not if they're left alone. If you use public transit, ask about their policies concerning pets. The Alaska State Ferry requires pets to remain in your vehicle, below the deck. Cats do well but dogs escape and often chew up the interiors of cars. I've driven thousands of miles with cats and flown my felines around the continent with no tranquilizers and no ill effects.

7

"Are We Settled Yet?"

Integration Phase
(After Six Months)

It's been six months. You've unpacked and rearranged the furniture. You know more about your long-term prospects as a resident of your new community. If you're lucky, you've met a few people who might become good friends someday. However, you may not feel at home in your new community for a long time.

It Takes Time to Feel at Home

Jan was sitting in her favorite coffee shop at the mall, skimming the local paper. She had just joined a jewelry design class and was beginning to feel busy for the first time since moving to Midwood. Jan felt even more at home when Roselyn from her aerobics class asked if she could share her table, as the café was crowded.

"So how are you enjoying the city?" Roselyn asked.

"Let's see, it's been . . . hmm, six months!" Jan said. "And mostly I like it a lot. There's plenty to do. But it's taking some time to meet people."

"Of course," said Roselyn, calmly sipping her coffee. "At least ten years to make friends."

"Ten years!" Jan gasped. She'd be ready for retirement by then! And then Jan was struck by a reassuring thought: "It's not something *I'm* doing wrong!"

Jan *was* doing everything right. She had joined a health club, attended PTA meetings, and introduced herself to the neighbors. But Midwood presented special challenges. Most of the community had grown up in Midwood and stayed close to their families. And now that she thought about it, Jan realized, most newcomers talked about moving away.

Because of her children and her husband's career, Jan couldn't leave Midwood for at least another three years. While she was relieved to learn she was doing nothing wrong, she couldn't help wondering if she should continue to put more effort into what now appeared to be a hopeless cause. What would she do for the next three years?

"Why Does It Take So Long?"

Researchers consistently find that people need to live in a location at least two years before they feel at home. Midwood's ten-year gap is exceptional, but it's by no means unique. People like to spend time with others like themselves. When you're new, you represent an unfamiliar quantity and may appear to have little in common with your new neighbors. You're a stranger here.

People often judge strangers more harshly than they judge friends and relatives. Psychologists Murray and Holmes (1994) found that people in close relationships found ways to maintain friendships even when they obtained negative information about each other. For instance, you learn that "Frank has gotten overextended with debts," or, "Frank drank too much at the party last week." If you feel close to Frank, the research suggests, you will offset this information with positive stories: "Frank works very hard and he's been having a tough time with his children." If Frank is a stranger, you might decide that he's just a drunk and, therefore, he's not the kind of person you want for a friend.

People are more likely to maintain a *quid pro quo* relationship with strangers than with friends (Clark 1984). Your neighbor offers you a ride to the supermarket when your car won't start during your first cold winter. If you don't know each other well, you probably keep track of who did what for whom. You thank your new neighbor by bringing over a gift or offering to drive her to the airport next week. If you are friends, you'll probably say to yourself, "Who's counting?"

An offer of help from a friend or family member will usually be appreciated, but offers from more distant acquaintances may seem manipulative (Hobfoll and Stokes 1989). Does that offer of a ride on a cold day mean that you'll have to say yes when she asks you to baby-sit? Do your new neighbors regard your gift of a homemade cake with suspicion? These are common reactions when people are getting to know one another.

Research also provides hope for newcomers. Just "hanging in," as one newcomer wrote, can pay surprising dividends. Studying urban environments, psychologist Stanley Milgram (1977) reported that people seek out familiar faces, even among strangers they see each morning at a bus stop. People often prefer to exercise in health clubs where they see familiar faces, even if they don't talk to one another (Goodwin and Hill 1998). Many joggers report they sometimes wave to familiar strangers.

People tend to respond positively to people who seem familiar. "We attended the same church for three months," says Winifred, "and suddenly everyone was talking to us." People report similar experiences with health clubs, business groups, stores, even libraries.

You may feel invisible the first time you participate in a local activity. But the second time around, you'll reap big dividends. "The first time I signed up for pottery, everybody ignored me," reports Roxanne, a single woman in Chicago. "They all knew each other. They had lived here for years and they had been through watercolors, jewelry-making, even woodwork. But I just kept quiet and worked on my pots. So I signed up again in February and—wow! They greeted me like an old friend."

"If I Speed Up, I'll Get a Ticket."

Whether you're driving down the highway or settling into a new community, you will find that speeders pay a price. Bernice Pescosolido (1986), who has studied cross-cultural moves, found that newcomers sometimes demonstrate too much eagerness. Often they are too quick to try to join in with old-timers, who rebuff their efforts. Sometimes newcomers have to pay some form of "dues." Surviving a frigid winter or a blistering summer can be viewed as passing a test.

When Hiram and Alice moved to Alaska, they felt they had to cross an invisible barrier before they would be accepted. Finally, Hiram spoke with Kevin, who had moved "up here" four years ago. "People won't take you seriously the first year or two," Kevin explained, "because a lot of people move up here and then find they can't take the winters. They wait to see if you'll be around awhile."

"Will I Feel Like This Forever?"

By now you have passed through several phases of grief. You've said farewell (chapter 4) and you may still be dealing with homesickness (chapter 6). You might think, "It's been six months . . . or a year. I should be in good shape by now!" You've heard the saying, "Time heals all wounds," but grief follows its own timetable. Psychologists Tait and Silver (1989) have shown that people frequently revisit painful or embarrassing memories for many years afterward. You may experience unexpected sadness on special occasions. "During the first year, I did fine till Independence Day," said Ursula. "Our old neighborhood always held a big picnic. I found myself feeling really sad as July approached and I didn't know why. Then the kids asked, 'Will we have a big picnic this year?' And I suddenly realized I was grieving for the friends and the fellowship we'd always enjoyed on this holiday."

Real healing begins when you can find meaning in your loss by making something good come out of your transformation. This process cannot be rushed. Meaning will often emerge over time. There are many ways to find meaning in experience, including those listed below.

Help Others

Just as victims of crime often volunteer at crisis centers, you may find ways to help others speed their adjustment to your community. "I don't want anybody to go through what I did," says Mary. "When I moved here, nobody helped me. I was alone with a six-year-old daughter. Now when somebody joins our company, I call and offer to help. Sometimes they say, 'no, thanks,' but sometimes they appreciate the help. I'll take people to see apartments, show them around town, basically offer a shoulder to lean on. I feel like I'm saving lives."

See the World Differently

People who survive a serious illness or accident often report, "I see the world differently now. I appreciate what I have." Alan reported a change in perspective after he moved from Atlanta to Denver. "I hated Atlanta. I'm not a Southerner and I hated the heat and the crime. I couldn't wait to leave for the mountains. Now," he continues, "I love Denver, but I wish I'd taken more time to appreciate Atlanta. I keep reading about things I could have done and places I could have visited. There's so much Civil War history down there and there were some good museums and concerts I just ignored. Now I am taking time to study guidebooks about Denver. I may get transferred again and I want to enjoy everything while I can."

Honor What You Had

In *Transcending the Loss*, Ashley Prend (1997) reports that many people deal with the death of a loved one by being grateful for whatever time they had with the person who died. A year, five years—any amount of time is better than zero.

When you must leave a place you love, you can also express your appreciation. "I'm so grateful for my two years in San Francisco. Most people spend less than a week there and wish they could stay more." "I can't believe I got paid to move to Alaska. It was the trip of a lifetime." "I loved my rose garden in New England. I may never have another one." "When my husband was stationed in Germany, I traveled all over Europe. I've heard every orchestra and visited every museum, many times over. I will treasure those memories forever."

Expect to Heal as You Achieve a New Identity

Some researchers believe that the outcome of grief is not acceptance but a shift of identity (Silverman 1993). As your identity shifts from "former resident of . . ." to "current resident of . . ." your grief fades. "I took up horseback riding. That will always be part of my life." "I learned to appreciate opera by attending free concerts in the park. A whole new world has opened up." "Before we moved, I felt like a fifth wheel when I volunteered for the PTA. Now my kids attend a small school that really needs me!"

═══ Exercise ═══
Who Am I Now?

This exercise will help you understand how much—or how little—you have changed since you first began planning your move. In chapter 1, you wrote a series of "I am" statements to describe who you were. Do not turn back just yet. Instead go to a quiet place, where you will not be disturbed for an hour. Write down ten new "I am" statements.

1. I am _____

2. I am _____

3. I am _____

4. I am _____

5. I am _____

6. I am _____

7. I am _____

8. I am _____

9. I am _____

10. I am _____

Now return to the "I am" statements from chapter 1. What are the differences? How have you changed? Write a summary of the differences.

Rosemarie, who moved from Chicago to a suburb in upstate New York, wrote

I'm more into fitness and activity now. That's not really new—I played varsity basketball in college—but I got away from it in the city. I didn't realize how much I've come to value walking, playing tennis, and spending more time with the family. Before, when we lived in the city, I spent so much time commuting. Now I spend more time outdoors. I am more relaxed. Yes, I've grown, but I feel like I'm just rediscovering who I am.

Kevin, who moved from a small town in Pennsylvania to New York City, wrote

I don't have much time to think about things like this. I'm always off doing something. Most important, I've started painting again and on Saturday I go to the galleries—something I couldn't do before I moved. A lot of my statements are about being a painter, a creative person, a lover of life. Things will never be the same. I may never leave New York.

You may have difficulty writing anything positive. Theresa couldn't find anything good to say about her new residence:

I am miserable, angry, frustrated. This place sucks. There is nothing I enjoy doing here. Nothing works. People are rude. I feel that I am constantly compromising on everything: the quality of life, the children's school, the shopping. I want to get away as soon as possible. I am embarrassed to say I live here.

The following sections are designed to help you make progress through the next six months, whether you commit to the new community or commit to admitting you have made a mistake. Your "I am" statements and summary will give you a reference point as you begin to consolidate the building blocks of your new identity.

Building a New Identity

For your interim identity, chapter 6 recommended that you pack an Emotional First Aid Kit. Now you need serious survival gear.

Pack a Compass and Pick a Star

When you're sailing on the ocean, you can easily lose sight of your goal. The ocean is vast and pathways are not marked. Even with today's modern navigation equipment, sailors still learn to steer by the stars, in case all that sophisticated wizardry goes down. How can you choose a star to steer by? Begin by breaking down your time into three-month or six-month chunks. Two, three, or ten years will seem unmanageable, but six months will speed by.

The following exercises will help you create a positive growth experience for the next several months. True, you may be feeling pressured for time and money. True, you're still learning your way around. Still, these six months will contribute to the quality of your life for many years to come.

═══ Exercise ═══
Three Wishes

Your own personal genie appears and offers to grant you three wishes that will be manifested in six months. But you must be very specific in your requests. You can say, "I want a very tall boyfriend with a great sense of humor," but you can't just ask for love. You can say, "I want to complete six abstract watercolors," but you can't say, "I want to paint." You can say, "I want to spend three weeks on a Greek island," but you can't say, "I want to travel."

Wish 1: _____

Wish 2: _____

Wish 3: _____

After you've come up with three wishes, the genie says, "Oops, there's a catch. I forgot to tell you that you must spend the next six months living right here in your new location. You may travel, but your primary residence is here." How would you modify your wishes?

═ Exercise
Life or Death

Imagine that you have six months to live. You will be healthy during that time and your loved ones are provided for. How do you want to spend the next six months? What are some of the things you'd want to make time for? Make a list.

═ Exercise
Setting Goals

So what will you do for the next three months? For six months?

Using the previous two exercises as a guide, set some goals for the next few months. Yes, "getting out of here" is okay as a goal. For example:

Sign up the Mega Foods account for my firm.

Earn [choose dollar amount] from my part-time business.

Take a course in French and visit Paris.

Be able to run a mile in [choose a number] minutes.

Plant a garden.

Complete the first 100 pages of a novel.

Goal 1: _____

Goal 2: _____

and, if there's time left over:

Goal 3: _____

Develop at Least One Constructive Daily Practice

A constructive practice may be anything that honors who you are: meditation, walking, exercise, writing letters, keeping a journal. Ideally, such a practice will become a meaningful ritual, something you do every day or every week no matter where you are. A ritual should take no longer than twenty minutes: short enough to fit into your schedule, but long enough to have an impact on your life.

In her book *The Artist's Way*, Julia Cameron encourages her readers to write three pages of free association first thing every morning. Cameron also encourages a weekly creativity break. Visit an art museum, attend a concert, or buy some art materials and create something.

Give yourself twenty-one days to make this practice part of your new life. Getting started is like putting yourself on autopilot: you have to trust the process. Set your direction and think about what will help you get there. Then—just begin! If you practice your ritual for twenty-one days, without a break, you will find it becomes a part of your daily life.

Try to remain faithful to your practice once you've established it. Skipping even one day can disrupt the flow of energy you have generated through weeks of faithful adherence. Everyone needs to skip a day every now and then; don't scold yourself if you miss one day. Resuming a practice right after traveling tends not to be difficult, but if you've taken a break to make phone calls or watch a television program resuming may be a little tough. Do not judge yourself. Just resume your practice, gently, recognizing that you may have to use some willpower to get back in the groove.

Here are some practices that other newcomers have found successful during the first two years:

Affirmations: "Every morning, I wrote ten positive statements in longhand, and I repeated this practice in the evening. I repeated these statement for myself throughout the day to help me focus on what was important to me. One affirmation went, 'I have a warm and caring support group in this community.' And now I do!"

"I would write a paragraph of affirmation every morning as soon as I turned on the computer. After that, I felt that my new home was a place where wishes come true."

Meditation: "I use a mantra meditation, fifteen or twenty minutes a day. It relaxes me and I can take it anywhere."

Journal: "I started writing three pages a day after reading *The Artist's Way* and I've never stopped. Writing clears my head. At first I wrote all about my anger with the new place, but now I write about the things I enjoy."

Visualization: "I visualized myself in the Strawberry Hills neighborhood, living in a house with blue shutters with a creek in the back yard. I imagined terrific neighbors, a reading group that met every two weeks, and a new special friend to share my life with. It took two years, but it all happened. The house came up for sale just when I got my bonus at work."

Running: "A twenty-minute run each morning sets me up for the rest of the day."

Yoga: "I take a class once a week and work with a tape every day."

Design a Six-Month Creativity Project

You can draft a short novel or create a series of paintings in six months. You can learn several pieces of music. You will be different, and your life will be changed.

No time? No interest? Your project may grow out of your constructive practices. In fact, many people who begin running or journal-keeping are surprised to find energy bubbling up in seemingly unrelated areas of their lives. In their book, *The Artist's Way at Work,* Mark Bryan, Julia Cameron, and Catherine Allen recommended a twelve-week program to help you understand your own creativity. Your local community center, library, or psychology institute may sponsor a group that follows this program or a similar one.

When you're done, start another project. You may get hooked.

Risk a New Social Identity

While you need to focus first on building your self-concept, consider taking some risks as you feel stronger. Writing about cross-cultural moves, psychiatrist Carlos Sluzki (1986) advises people to anticipate loneliness, but also to take proactive steps to meet people. Newcomers who have been interviewed agree.

Meeting people does not mean that you call up strangers to invite them for lunch or coffee, although some newcomers have been successful with that approach. Meeting people means being available, making small talk, and letting yourself become what psychologist Stanley Milgram called a "familiar stranger." Attend meetings, classes, and groups. Participate carefully, realizing that old-timers may be wary of newcomers. Think of having fun, not making friends. A friendship should happen gradually, without effort. Don't force it.

Be a Tourist

You might be thinking, "I will never feel at home here." If that's the case, pretend to be a tourist or an anthropologist. Along the way, you may find yourself going native—a serious transgression among anthropologists, but an occasion for joy among newcomers to a community.

Tourists enjoy visiting a particular city, but don't identify themselves as residents. They buy sweatshirts with the local place name and fill their homes with souvenirs. They go sight-seeing. They gain confidence in their temporary roles, framing their experience as an adventure. Their friends are shipboard acquaintances. A pleasant evening? Great. For now, that's enough.

Tourists often experiment with temporary identities. Hal had just lost his lover. They had always been a serious, stay-at-home couple. When Hal moved to Chicago, he decided to try a new lifestyle, attending more parties and serving fewer dinners at home. He knew he wouldn't want to live this way forever, but he felt this temporary lifestyle would help him heal.

If you're on a short-term assignment, you may decide to go all out as a tourist: spend money on excursions, take extra trips to see friends, and generally try to make the most of a location that will not become home. This approach works well for many people.

If you're baffled by your new community and find yourself resisting its values, try becoming an anthropologist for a while. Instead of the celebratory attitude, you can try the investigative. Anthropologists investigate. They may never be part of the local scene, but they want to gain deeper insights by studying it. Each person is viewed as an informant, a source of information. Anthropologists go home and write field notes, summarizing their observations. They're objective and analytical. They may have less fun than the tourists, but they can often come away with profound new perspectives. They also spend a lot less money.

Acknowledge Resistance

Even the most dedicated newcomers can become exasperated with their new community. Nearly everyone says at some point, "I wish I'd never heard of this place!" You may feel helpless, even violated. Eleanor Adaskin (1987) studied executives forced to relocate and found that feelings of helplessness often translated to anger and resentment.

Some people just have trouble letting go of their previous identity. Dan says, "I still miss my life in San Francisco. It's like falling in love and breaking up before you're ready. You can't just grab a new person to take their place." Dan left California to attend graduate school in Chicago. For three years, he wore Bermuda shorts through Chicago's fabled winters. Eventually, he became more comfortable with the city. Last I heard, he even owned a parka.

You're Getting Restless

Do you have a pattern of restlessness? You may be setting impossible goals as a way to avoid confronting deeper issues. Or you may just be someone who likes mobility, like Richard Ford who wrote about his experiences for *Harper's* (see chapter 1). People who are resistant to settling down often achieve career and life satisfaction when assigned to jobs calling for a lot of travel. Others thrive on relocating every two years.

You Don't Get Along with Your House

In her book, *House as a Mirror of Self,* Clare Cooper Marcus (1995) asked people to think about their homes in a new way, entering into a dialogue with their dwelling places. Some people felt their homes welcomed and enjoyed them. Some felt the opposite. One woman in particular really hated her house. After a brief dialogue, she realized the feeling was mutual: the house was equally unhappy to have her there.

═ Exercise ═══════════════════
Dialogue with Your Dwelling

Choose a time when you can be alone and undisturbed. Allow yourself to experience being in your house or apartment. Walk around and appreciate what is there, then get comfortable and close your eyes.

Imagine that you are talking to your house.

What would you like to tell the house? How does the house respond?

How does the home see you? Are you a welcome guest or an intruder?

What does the house expect from you? How can you make the house more of a home?

What do you want the house to do for you? Why does the house resist becoming a home?

Marcus used a similar approach to gather data for her research and found it yielded deep emotional responses, sometimes joyous, sometimes painful. Marcus writes that she took care to follow up with people who experienced strong reactions, making sure they were not alone. If you find yourself becoming distressed, stop the exercise. You may want to explore your feelings with a trusted friend or counselor.

Your Home Can Grow on You

After moving from Dallas, Helen's first letters from Seattle were filled with anguish: "I hate it here. There's too much rain." Within a year, she was writing, "I can't imagine living anywhere else!" What happened? Helen isn't sure. She didn't realize she'd become a convert until she flew to Dallas for a wedding. "It's so flat here!" she exclaimed. "I never noticed! And there are no mountains!"

Acknowledge That Your New Identity May Be Between Two Worlds

In a *New York Times* essay, Linda Carroll Martin (1998) wrote that she still missed New York City after eight years in Cincinnati. She even missed being able to complain—the New Yorker's favorite pastime! She confesses being torn between the two cities. When she visits family in New York, she's still confused as to whether she's traveling to or from her home.

"We used to live in upstate New York," said Burt. "Now we live in Philadelphia. We still don't feel at home here. But when we go back to upstate New York, we have no ties anymore."

Keep a Logbook

Mark Milestones

Keep track of experiences when you feel at home in the new community, even if they seem trivial. This experience can be fueled by a chance remark. I can remember when someone referred to "the Kenwood store" and I knew just where it was. Notice when you become a "regular" at a store or a restaurant. When you ask for something extra, do the servers tend to say yes more often? Do you receive unexpected coupons or bonuses? One coffee shop handed out Christmas cards with coupons to regulars—a special treat for newcomers.

Track Phone Calls

Do you find yourself calling "home" less often? Are you socializing with people who live in your new city? Notice who you call when you want to share good news or recover from bad news.

Record Your Reactions to Visits Home

Linda Carroll Martin (1998), the writer who still misses New York after eight years in Cincinnati, admits she now becomes annoyed with New Yorkers who express dismay at the frigid climate of Ohio. Cincinnati's climate, she insists, is not that different from Manhattan's.

Moving Tip

Pack the Essentials

When you leave for your new location, take the essentials with you: toilet paper, garbage bags, and paper towels. Yes, you can pick them up easily, but you won't feel like heading for the grocery store as soon as you arrive. Also, pack telephone directories—white and yellow pages—from your former city. You may need to track down an elusive shop or an important service provider.

8

"I Live Here Now . . ."

The Maintenance Phase

If you're still here after two years, your conversations will reflect the way you've accepted a new identity. You may talk about the good weather "we've" been having, or the weeks of below-forty temperature that "they" have around here. You may talk about "our" museums and galleries or you may have difficulty switching allegiance to "their" local sports teams. You may find yourself rejoicing for your new identity, grieving for what you've given up, or striving to balance the different components of your new identity.

Rejoicing

"We've never looked back," says Carole. "Coming here was like coming home." For Carole and her family, the move offered a continuation of their identity. The new location afforded numerous opportunities for self-expression: art lessons for a creative teenager, varsity swimming for a budding athlete, and fulfilling professional associations for the adults.

June, who had never been married, began to discover the benefits of stability. She had moved around the country, changing jobs and cities every two or three years. When she moved to Chicago, she lucked into a good job as a retail merchandiser and she began dating a "very special man." June's college roommate, passing through on a business trip, exclaimed, "I can't believe you've lived here five years!" The time had sped by. June had put together a network of friends who provided social support.

What surprised her was the change to her paper identity. "Your credit rating improves automatically if you stay in one place," she says, still amazed. "Suddenly it was easy to get credit anywhere. My checks and my driver's license matched for the first time and I didn't even think about it. I knew just where to shop for a party or a gift. My vet would board the cat at a moment's notice and the mechanic gave me a ride home when my car broke down in the middle of the day. This never happened when I was moving around."

Ongoing Grief

For some people, their new residence offers daily reminders of a loss of their self-concept. This kind of grief can be compared to the sadness felt in response to other losses that are mourned over a lifetime. A widower told sociologist Robert Weiss (1990, 6), "You don't get over it; you get used to it." These losses cause considerable pain because you are losing something that is a critical part of your identity. You feel that you actually are losing part of yourself. "I'm a Southern boy living in Massachusetts," says Ralph. "I live here but I'll never be a New Englander. My roots are in Birmingham, and in Mississippi where I went to school."

Some people feel happy most of the time, but then they're hit by unexpected pangs of grief. You may discover a lost aspect of your self-concept that suddenly seems crucial to your well-being. Claire moved to Boise two years ago: "When I visited my sister in Seattle, I realized how much I needed the excitement of a big city. I haven't felt so alive in months." Patricia, after eighteen months working in Tulsa, felt the same way: "I almost cried when I got off the phone with my old roommate, Leslie. I hadn't realized how much I wanted to be around people like me."

For other newcomers, awareness grows slowly. Looking back over the years, you realize, "I've never quite made this adjustment." Ken moved to northern Florida from Wisconsin. "You know what I miss most?" he says. "Exercise! For the last five years, a group of us guys would go down to the college gym at lunch and play basketball. I'd go for hikes on weekends. Well, I've lived down here almost six years and I just haven't found a group of guys who get together for basketball. And you just can't hike during the Florida summers."

An activity as simple as basketball has made a big difference in Ken's life. Lacking his favorite exercise, he's gained weight and feels self-conscious about it. After four years in Florida, Ken hasn't been able to replace a significant aspect of his self-concept.

Seasonal Grief

Some people insist they feel thoroughly acclimated, but find themselves experiencing sudden, often surprising, waves of grief. These emotions are often triggered by symbols that hold special meaning, long after people have moved to a new city: "We used to be able to cut down our own Christmas tree," or, "Spring in the country, when you'd see the first crocus."

People who move to warm locations, such as Florida or southern California, often are surprised to realize how much they miss the seasonal changes of their former lives. "Last October, I was typing up promotional copy for Thanksgiving," said Naomi. "I was working late in the Miami office and when I walked out the door, I got hit with a blast of hot, humid air. Suddenly I felt so homesick! I'd expected to see trees with the leaves turning colors, and here were all these palm trees in the parking lot." After five years in San Diego, "I never thought I'd miss the cold, but I could use a real snowstorm about now," a retiree told me wistfully.

Sorting Out Your Ambivalence

Many people experience some ambivalence in their adopted homes, even occasional grief, but feel no need to explore their feelings further. But what if you get a call out of the blue asking you if you would like to move again? Or maybe you just decide you want a better understanding of your relationship to your environment.

Exercise
I Don't Feel at Home

"I've been here awhile, but I don't feel at home." Does this describe your feelings about where you live? If so, take a few minutes and ask yourself the following questions:

- "What am I feeling here?"
- "What is missing?"
- "When do I feel happy here?"
- "When do I feel sad?"

You may want to write down your answers so you can review them later. Based on the answers to these four questions, what is your relation to your residence now? What image or metaphor comes to mind?

Honoring Your Loss

"Just don't think about it." That's what Lenora's sister said at Christmas. "You've got a great job. You like being outdoors, you don't miss fighting the traffic, and your neighbors are terrific. So why worry about coffee or being near the ocean? You never went to the beach anyway!"

Leonora tried, yet she found herself restless and edgy for reasons she did not understand. She made friends, but something was missing. Lenora was not allowing herself to grieve. She missed being able to express herself by long walks by the sea, or by leisurely afternoons sipping espresso while she planned the novel she would write someday. Unexplained feelings, such as irritability and tension, are often the result of unrecognized grief.

Here are some steps to help you identify the source of your feelings more clearly.

Acknowledge Your Losses

If you keep a journal, you may want to record your feelings as they arise. "I used to take art classes in the evening, but there just isn't any way I can paint or draw here." "I could walk to work. It was a two-mile walk and I would watch the seasons change. Now I drive in an air-conditioned car." "I miss my friends. They went to the same kind of high school and college that I did. We spoke the same language."

Identify the Meaning of Your Loss

It can be helpful to try to come up with an image of your feelings. Think about your loss and imagine a metaphor that describes it. Draw the image. It could be "something being pulled from me," or "a candle being blown out," or perhaps "a hole in a tree."

Seek Images of Nourishment, Healing, and Repair

When you lose parts of your identity, you may experience a feeling of emptiness. This emptiness can be viewed as a form of hunger, or a hole in your identity that needs to be mended.

At first you may have difficulty recapturing what you have lost. Some friends urged Jeanne to be creative at home, but she really missed having a special place to go, like the art studio in her old school. What she can do is acknowledge the loss and look for ways to repair it by bringing creativity back into her life.

Because you might not know what's available, you will often have trouble identifying specific things you can do to heal your loss. By keeping yourself open to experience, you will find yourself drawn to meaningful experiences that will lead to healing and repair.

What Next?

Now that you've settled in, you may decide, "This is it! I will never move again!" On the other hand, you may be a multiple mover, by necessity or design. In either case, you can prepare yourself by taking steps to protect your identity.

"I'll Never Move Again!"

If you're absolutely determined to remain where you are, put down roots as soon as possible. But remember, any forecast can be altered by unexpected events. You may want to reduce the chance of relocation by preparing for possible turbulence.

Begin by considering what might force a new move. If your response focuses on career issues, begin to explore alternative places of employment. You may have to make compromises with your career identity in order to maintain your identity as "resident of . . ." Remember Elaine in chapter 1? She realized she would have to seek career alternatives if she wanted to be sure she could remain in Boston. Do not wait until you are faced with another relocation. Do the research now so you will be prepared for a possible upheaval. Here are some questions you should think about:

- If you work for someone else, what could you do as an independent contractor?

- How will you obtain health insurance? In Philadelphia the Chamber of Commerce offers health insurance to qualified entrepreneurs.

You may find options through national professional associations or local entrepreneurship groups.

* How can you network in your community so you will know about new opportunities if they should arise?

* Have you considered starting a new career? Now that you've established residency you may be eligible for tuition discounts at local universities.

Family pressure can be considerably more difficult to plan for. Many people are forced to move because of family reasons. These moves are especially difficult because you lose your identity as a "resident of" as well as your career identity. A child may need to attend a special school, and the whole family follows. Perhaps an aging relative needs help and the whole family needs to move to provide a closer source of support.

An important question to ask yourself in these situations is, "Do I really *need* to move?" More than one family has discovered after the fact that they didn't need to go: "We thought we were helping, but they really didn't need us there." Maybe the family member can move here? Your child could attend a boarding school or live with a local family. Consider all the alternatives before volunteering to give up a location that you've grown to love.

After exhausting all of the possibilities, you may find that you have no choice; you have to move. If this is the case, here are some suggestions to prepare for your next Big Move.

"I Live Here Now—but I Have to Move Again!"

You may discover that you work for a company that encourages frequent transfers. You've finally gotten settled, and it's time to move again. How can you prepare yourself?

Self-Concept: What Can You Do Anywhere?

You've already seen how the self-concept can be expressed through activities and rituals. You want to develop self-contained activities that define your self-concept wherever you are. "Avoid classes," advises Judith, a multiple mover, "and find things you enjoy to doing at home. I have my gardening and I just began making jewelry. Classes are nice, but you can't count on having them available. I started doing pottery and the next place we moved didn't have a school with a studio." "Reading and music," says Richard, a single man. "And my dog." "Our family makes Sunday a special day," says Alan. "Wherever we are, we try to do something together on Sunday afternoons or we all go to the movies on Sunday night."

You can also express your self-concept through possessions. As you buy furniture and specialty items for your house or office, allow your choice to be influenced by your future move. "I try not to buy anything I'll have to leave behind," says Yvonne. "These days almost anything can fit into a moving van, but someday I may have to move myself." "The cats come with us everywhere," says Neville. "They transform even a temporary living space into a real home." "I won't move into a place that clashes with my room-size rug," says June. "It changes the appearance of the room and makes me feel at home."

Social Identity: Who Can You Talk to Anywhere?

Today's electronic options allow you to maintain ties with friends and family all over the world. E-mail is easy, cheap, and fun. An e-mail message is no substitute for a hug, but a message can remind you that you are still thought of as a caring friend and family member. Begin to assemble your network while you are still here, creating a sort of social identity insurance.

Consider joining professional associations or other groups with national memberships. Many people reinforce their social identity when they meet people from a new branch of their national organization.

Paper Identity: "Where Can I Cash a Check?"

Protecting a paper identity requires you to remain aware of how you appear on paper. When you move again, you'll be scrutinized by banks, utility companies, and other agencies. Keep your documents organized. When you move, you'll need to assemble information about your insurance and your finances. If you own a home, you'll have to produce deeds, title insurance, and more. Organizing your family's medical records—even your pet's medical records—can save a great deal of time and aggravation when it's time to pull up stakes again.

====== **Internet Moving Tip** ======

Right on Red?

Before you move, you can learn about the motor vehicle code of your new state. Entering "Florida Motor Vehicles" in my search engine produced a guide to DMV locations, and a list of required documents. Many driver handbooks are now online so you can study for the written test before you leave. Few states or provinces require you to take a new test these days, as long as your license is current.

PART 3

Special Situations

9

"This Is NOT Who I Am!"

Resisting a New Identity

You may have read the story of the FBI agent who sold classified information to the former Soviet Union. When asked why he betrayed his country, he told the media that he resented his transfer to New York. He hated the crime, the noise, the crowds, and the cost of living. Feeling betrayed by his assignment, he betrayed his employer, the United States Government.

This reaction may seem unusually strong, but people can have intense emotional responses to their locations. Newcomers are often reluctant to admit how much they hate a new location. Those who turn to others for help often receive little support. Well-meaning people offer comments like "I could live anywhere and be happy," or "People are the same wherever you go."

Encountering Resistance

The reality is that many researchers and practicing therapists have come to believe that some places can be all wrong for some people.

When I interviewed·Joan Lerner, a psychologist in private practice in Philadelphia, she said that some people simply are not suited to a particular location. Even the weather, she says, can affect adjustment to a new area.

So why do people relocate to environments where they will be miserable?

"I Need to Make a Living."

You may have a conflict between your career options and your lifestyle preferences. "The kind of selling I do," said Neville, "involves building a relationship with my clients. I like working with businesses that have been around and plan to stay around. This Sunbelt city is just too transient. Everybody just arrived. I love the lifestyle, but I can't make a living."

Andrea had lived in the same city for twenty years and she loved it. When she was laid off, however, she felt she had to move. "The economy here is going downhill and there aren't any jobs," she said. "Companies are moving out of the city." With great reluctance, Andrea moved to a small city in upstate New York. "There's nothing I enjoy doing on the weekends, but I'm staying afloat professionally," she said.

"I Didn't Know Better."

Some newcomers realize they did not obtain enough information about their new location. "I always assumed people would be friendly here," said Ruth, who had just moved to a city in the Rocky Mountain area. "I didn't realize it would be so cold so early in the year. It was my own fault. I didn't do my research. I just read some novels set in this city and talked to a few people who lived here ten years ago."

Jed, on the other hand, felt he was deliberately misled by his employer and the realtor who came highly recommended. "We specifically asked about the history of this condo complex," he said. "We knocked on a couple of doors and the neighbors seemed okay. Right after we moved in we learned there were all kinds of property damage, break-ins and lawsuits, and everybody knew about it. The local name for the property was Mondo Condo. It was on the front page of the paper just a few months before we started looking. I did read the last month of the local paper, but I'd just missed the story."

While Ruth may come to appreciate her new city, Jed will probably continue to feel betrayed. "Next time," he says, "I'll get more references from the realtor, but at some point you have to assume people are what they claim to be. And this guy was recommended by my boss, so I don't really want to sue him."

"Maybe There's Something Wrong with Me."

Sometimes your discontent with a location reflects discontent with yourself. If you find yourself unhappy after two or three moves, you may want to ask, "Is it me or is it the locations?" You may find that you have chosen a series of locations that are, in fact, all wrong for you. You may be hard to please or you may have inadvertently made a vocational choice that limits your lifestyle options. You need to clarify your career and life objectives before making yet another futile move.

In a study of life transitions, psychologist Morton Lieberman (1992) found that some people have an easier time making smooth transitions to new identities, while others have more difficulty with change. The difference seems to depend on the way people interpret life transitions. People who were able to maintain a consistent self-concept functioned more effectively than those who changed their self-concept to fit the situation.

"I moved several times for a new job," says Frieda. "Each time I thought I'd caught the brass ring. The last move taught me a lesson. I loved living in Chicago, but I was still miserable. The company offered me the best options in my field, but I was still frustrated. It's not the city, it's the job. I am now investigating a new career or even starting my own business."

Todd's conflict was nearly opposite to Frieda's. Todd teaches art history at the college level. Although jobs in that field are very scarce, Todd has managed to obtain full-time positions at four different schools for the last ten years. "I've paid a price, though," he says. "I've hated every place I've lived. Colleges tend to be located in small towns and the jobs on the East Coast are especially hard to get.

"At first," Todd said, "I thought it was me. I'd get tense and irritable and take it out on my family. But my wife pointed out that I was relaxed and happy when I had access to the museums and the galleries and city life in general." Todd has decided to investigate ways to combine his interest in art with some business courses, perhaps setting up a business to help corporations purchase art work.

"I Never Wanted to Come Here in the First Place!"

After Frank finished graduate school in Kansas, he accepted a job in Wisconsin. He and his family settled comfortably into small town life. Unfortunately, Frank's nonprofit agency lost a major grant and funding was tight. Frank's wife couldn't find a job. After five years, the family reluctantly decided they should move, and Frank accepted a better-paying job in Iowa. Frank writes, "Moving to Iowa was a much tougher move than when we moved to Wisconsin. While I was going to school in Kansas, we knew we would move. It was really something we were looking forward to—a positive transition. But our move to Iowa was a parallel move—lots of trade-offs: some things better, some things worse. There was much more conflict over whether we were doing the right thing."

For every kind of life transition, research consistently demonstrates that people respond more favorably when they feel they had a choice. If you felt forced to move, you may find yourself rebelling. It's normal to resist a situation where you seem to have no choice. "I won't go quietly! If I'm dragged across the state line, I'll be kicking and screaming!" You may be far too well-bred to show your anger, let alone kick and scream, but people often throw internal tantrums as they resist their new homes. If you feel you moved even though you didn't want to, it's important that you clarify your reasons for making this move. Each person is different and each situation must be evaluated individually. You may find the following exercise helpful in getting to the heart of your individual situation.

═══ **Exercise** ═══════════════════════════════
Why Am I Here?

Fill in the blanks:

I moved here because _____

_____

_____

I expected the people to be _____

_____

_____

I thought I would be able to _____

_____

_____

When I moved my possessions into my new home, _____

_____

_____

I am glad I was warned about _____

_____

_____

I wish I had been warned about _____

_____

_____

When I asked the local residents for information, they _____

_____

_____

Brian, who moved to a Southwestern suburb to keep his job, had the following answers:

I moved here because otherwise I'd lose my job.

I expected the people to be friendly and they were—but they asked me all kinds of personal questions.

I thought I would be able to get everything I needed here—and I can, but I have to drive twenty miles to get it.

When we moved our possessions into the house, they didn't fit. The pictures looked funny on the walls. We'll have to get a new couch.

I am glad I was warned about the weather. It wasn't so bad.

I wish I had been warned about the neighborhood. The school system isn't very good and there is no place for the kids to play together.

When I asked the local residents for information, they all smiled and said, "Everybody likes it here." It was tough to get information.

Julie, who just moved from Chicago to a small town in Virginia, had different responses:

I moved here to be closer to my parents, who are getting old. I wanted to be near family again.

I expected to enjoy the countryside and the outdoors—but I miss the city.

I thought I would be able to find a good job, but I'm taking a 20 percent pay cut and my career has been set back at least five years—if I still have a career.

When I moved my possessions into the condo I rented, I felt cramped. My old place was huge, with high ceilings and built-in shelves. I have to give away half of what I own, or pay for storage.

I am glad I was warned about the attitude toward anyone who's different. When my good friend who's African-American came to visit, we were ready for their reaction.

I wish I had been warned about the economy. I never should have bought this condo.

When I asked the local residents for information, they didn't look happy to see me. I should have been warned.

Both Brian and Julie have begun to understand what forces brought them to their new location. Now they need to understand why they are resisting and what they can do.

Reasons for Resisting

There are many reasons why you may not feel comfortable in your new location. In order to take steps to deal with your resistance, it's important that you get clear on exactly why you feel hostility about your new surroundings. Sometimes just realizing the source of your anxiety can make you feel a whole lot better.

"I Hate Being the Only One"

Chapters 2 and 3 encourage you to explore whether you can express your identity in your new destination. Sometimes you may be unable to express your identity because there is nobody around to understand it. Perhaps you're the only person of color, gay person, or childless person in the neighborhood. Those who live in your new community may not be aware of your isolation. You may face barriers that are invisible to most of the community.

Harold, an African-American who holds two graduate degrees, accepted a well-paying position with a firm in a conservative Southern city that was experiencing rapid economic growth. He could easily afford to live in an affluent suburb that gave him a pleasant ten-minute commute from his job.

Harold was shocked when he answered the door to accept delivery of his new sofa from a local department store. Looking past Harold, the driver asked, "Is he home?" "It never occurred to the driver that I might live there," Harold said later. "The driver figured this black guy at the door must be a servant. That was my moment of truth.

"I tried to tell myself that one negative experience might not be typical of an entire town. But then there was the dinner at a country club with some clients and partners from the firm. All the waiters were black and the guests were white, except for me. I just did not feel at home."

Explaining yourself on a regular basis is exhausting. Being a "first" or an "only" can be frustrating. Feeling isolated can seem intolerable. When you feel isolated, it's natural to resent those who seem to be placing you on an island.

"They'll never accept Rhoda and me as a couple," said Cecilia. "And it's just not worth the effort to keep trying."

"I just want to be around people like me," says Josh, who grew up in a Jewish household in New York. "People who understand what my home life was like, who don't even notice my accent, who have read the same books."

Most people realize that they can be isolated on the basis of race, religion, nationality, or sexual orientation. Yet isolation can be far more subtle.

George says, "Every time people see our house they say, 'Oh, you have so many books!' Back home in the college town where I grew up, our walls were lined with bookshelves. And people get so involved in their houses here! We can't invite people over until everything looks perfect."

Differences that seem trivial may affect the way you express your self-concept in the new location. Antoinette had become a broccoli-loving vegetarian in California. In her new home in the Rust Belt, she was horrified to learn that her host did not feel obliged to offer guests a vegetarian choice. "My friends in California would never serve a roast without checking with everybody ahead of time!" she exclaimed. "Red meat as the only option? Never!"

Her new friends thought she was weird. "You just eat it," they shrugged. "It's no big deal."

"I'm Embarrassed to Tell People I Live Here!"

You may feel that accepting your new home will force you to accept an identity that you don't feel comfortable with. Resistance to a new location can begin with a refusal to allow your self-concept to include "resident of . . ." You may not be comfortable saying, "I live in Littletown," or, "I live in Manhattan." Sometimes these places evoke negative images for you, images that have deep roots in childhood values.

"When I was growing up on a farm, we always made fun of people from the big city," says Ralph. "City folk seemed ignorant and . . . well, stupid. They couldn't find their way around a barn. Now here I am in Chicago and I'm supposed to stay at least three years. My wife and I are going nuts." Ralph's self-concept rebelled against saying, "I am from Chicago." He even had trouble saying, "We're living in Chicago now." Like many people, he was responding not only to his own doubts and worries, but also to the imagined doubts and worries of his friends and neighbors back home—an important part of his social identity. "What would they say if they saw me walking down Michigan Avenue in this suit? I always swore I'd never live where I couldn't grow things."

Sometimes real voices join the chorus of discomfort. When Daphne moved to Winnipeg, a city in the center of Canada known for flat prairies and freezing winters, her friends from Toronto were horrified. "They refused to visit," she reports. "They'd say, 'Why would anyone want to move to Winnipeg?'" Daphne had resisted the move and these friends confirmed her worst fears: she lived in a horrible place. Morton Lieberman (1996) notes that identity is confirmed by others who act as mirrors. Daphne's mirrors refused to reflect a positive image of herself as a person who belonged in Winnipeg.

Over time, these feelings may become more rather than less intense. If you hate where you live, your self-concept may become increasingly negative, leading to lower self-esteem. As you feel worse about yourself, you may resist taking actions that will improve your situation. Thus you create a self-fulfilling prophecy.

"Am I the Problem?"

"I feel like I'm being punished. I've been banished to the middle of nowhere." These messages imply a negative self-concept: "If I'm here, I must be a bad person."

You may feel that you are taking "a big step backward," as Jennifer said. "I started out in a town like this. I worked like a dog so I'd never have to come back. And now here I am again." Jennifer didn't say, "I'm a failure," but she felt like one.

What's happening? Your brain is working very hard to create a negative self-concept. These thoughts come from what McKay and Fanning (1992) call the Inner Critic, creator of the negative thoughts that float to the surface when you need them the least. When you are feeling tired and frustrated, you can expect to experience even more negative thoughts than usual. You put yourself down: "I'm so stupid! I should have known," in a sense declaring, "I'm incompetent! I can't get out of this mess." And with this mindset, you can't.

If you've just moved, you will be especially vulnerable to your Inner Critic. When you're feeling at home, you can recognize when the Critic exaggerates: "I don't always screw up. Just sometimes, just like everybody else in the world." In your new location you may not have a support structure to keep you in touch with your strengths; you don't know what's real and what's imaginary. The situation can seem hopeless.

In order to keep yourself in touch with your strengths, you need do a reality check when the Inner Critic comes to call. Here are some reality checks to help keep you on track.

Self-Concept Check: "I Don't Like the Person I'm Turning Into!"

Review your "I am" statements from chapter 1 and from chapter 7. Are there large discrepancies? Do you feel that your self-concept has changed drastically? Studies of people going through transitions show that those who undergo numerous changes to their self-image often have difficulty functioning effectively (Lieberman 1996). Sometimes your new location will be so different that you simply cannot express who you are.

Ralph and JoEllen offer particularly strong examples of people who need very specific settings to express their identities. Ralph belongs to two nature conservation groups and a bird-watching club. He spent two years in the Peace Corps, and his vacations are usually spent camping, fishing, and scuba diving. Ralph likes space and would probably have a hard time adapting to city living. JoEllen is the opposite. An artist and a vegetarian, she enjoys the anonymity of urban life and everyday access to the art world.

Other needs are more subtle. It's common for people not to realize what they needed until they lost it. Brenda, a freelance web page designer, moved to a charming college town in order to be closer to her fiancé. Soon she was asking herself, "Do I want to marry this guy if we have to live here?" Brenda's fiancé was a prominent administrator at the college that dominated the town, "so everybody knew him and soon everybody knew everything about me, too. We have no privacy here. And when he works late, there's nothing for me to do." Worst of all, Brenda says, "Last week I finished a big project and I wanted to celebrate. In Washington, I could choose from hundreds of restaurants and follow up with theater, concerts, anything. In the country I could go horseback riding or hiking. Here there's nothing."

=== Exercise ===
Just Deserts

People often reveal their values by the way they choose to reward themselves and the way they seek support when they feel sad or hurt. When these choices are limited, your identity will be interrupted. Getting clear about how you reward yourself can help you find ways to support your self-concept.

• How do you like to reward yourself for a job well done?

• How do you comfort yourself when you're hurt or anxious?

• How do you recover from a loss?

• What can you do here? What is missing?

When you start to hear the Critic whispering in your ear, think about treating yourself to something special. There is no better treatment for negativity than a good dose of enjoyment.

Social Identity Check: "The Neighbors Don't Seem to Like Me"

Prejudiced, cruel, insensitive people can be found anywhere, but there is no denying that certain prejudices may be more openly expressed and tolerated in some locations than in others. You may feel self-conscious in some communities if you're the Only One, but in others you are truly isolated. Helena, who is East Indian, found herself responding to insults from new neighbors who thought she was an Iranian terrorist. George decided not to move to a college town even though it was noted for its liberal attitudes. "They may be tolerant of different religions and races," he said, "but a few people openly made jokes about gay men and lesbians. My partner and I couldn't live together openly." June, who is Korean, married Kevin, an Irish-American. "In some cities," June says, "that's a mixed marriage. And in some cities, we can't rent an apartment together."

Some communities resist all newcomers, regardless of their race, religion, or sexual orientation. You may have found a location where there is little migration, where most of the residents have been around since they were born. People who rarely meet newcomers often resist making friends with new residents. Often their resistance is unconscious and has nothing to do with who you are. It's just that they evaluate you by the way you answer the question, "Where did you go to high school?"

"I was invited to attend a dinner at a local arts organization," Belinda recalls ruefully. "Here were all these people in their thirties, forties, and fifties, well-dressed, obviously affluent and successful. After all these years, people wanted to sit with their old high school buddies. I felt like I was attending somebody else's high school reunion."

While some newcomers may be oversensitive or may misinterpret their new surroundings, I have found that most people move with a positive attitude. They really try to fit in and are disappointed and hurt when they cannot be successful.

Large cities offer more transient populations, but newcomers will encounter resistance simply because people are busy and competition, even for social time, can be fierce. People tend to work long hours, reserving their free time for family. There are simply more people, all seeking similar social outlets. "Back home," said Edward, "I was sought after by every civic group in town. I was always giving talks and serving on committees with the most prominent people in town. Back home, I was on the board of the symphony. Here, I can't even get good seats."

═══ Exercise ═══
Social Reality Test

Complete the following sentences:

I feel isolated when I hear people say . . . _____

_____

_____

I feel isolated when people act . . . _____

_____

_____

_____

If you've made a friend or found someone at work you feel comfortable talking to, ask them what they think of your observations. Do they agree with your descriptions of what happened? What do they say about newcomers? _____

_____

_____

_____

Here are some answers offered by others.

My neighbor said, "You're right. We don't invite new people to our parties. We like to keep to ourselves."

My new friend at church told me I've got a tough road to hoe. She said they don't care much for black people around these parts. And someone at work said women don't last long.

I guess I was being too sensitive. We didn't realize they had been through a fire and a bitter divorce and they just didn't want to talk to anybody.

===

Paper Identity Check: "What Do I Have to Do for a Little Service?!"

Even your paper identity may begin to crumble when you don't fit comfortably into your new location. Chapter 4 noted that housing cultures differ across the country. In some locations, neighbors interact socially; in others, residents don't know who lives next door to them. Some regions place a great deal of importance on finicky housekeeping; others accept layers of dust as inevitable and expect you to live amidst clutter. Service available from your landlord and the building staff will vary a great deal, as will the amount you are expected to tip for such service. Expectations about noise levels, dog walking, garbage disposal, and lawn care all vary as you move.

If you're moving from a community where rents are low and housing is readily available, you may be horrified to find yourself dealing with landlords who seem to be looking for reasons to drive you away. A "standard lease" varies from state to state and even city to city. If you buy a house, you may find yourself in a situation that you never planned for. Some locales offer homeowners a gated community, where residents attend meetings and share costs of security service. You may find this style of living friendly, cooperative, and reassuring; or you may feel stifled.

You need time to learn the local style of doing business. Annette became increasingly frazzled as she dealt with one company after another, getting her car fixed and her home refurbished. "They show up late and they don't care." Annette's neighbors offered no sympathy: "That's just the way things are. Get used to it."

Exercise
Consumer Culture

Communities have cultures surrounding the way they do business. The following questions should help you get in touch with what's out there.

- How would you describe your new community's culture? Laid-back? Rigid?

- How do your neighbors and acquaintances respond when you describe your experiences?

- Does their response differ from yours?

Gina was used to the cold efficiency of her big city services, and was frustrated with what she found in her new town. She wrote:

This town has charm, and charm translates to inefficiency. You're always getting the wrong order in restaurants and repair people show up an hour late if they show up at all. That's the culture: laid back but no sense of service.

When I talked to the women in my aerobics class, they shrugged. What's the big deal? they laughed. What's your hurry?

What's worst of all is that nobody here ever complains about anything. They won't send food back. They never refuse to pay. So I come across as a bitch, and all I want is decent service.

Gina appears headed on a collision course with her new community. Her comments suggest a clash between values that will be difficult to overcome.

By reviewing what you learned from your reality checks, you should be able to focus on what specifically bothers you about your new environment. Now you need to ask yourself, "What can be changed?" and of the things that cannot be changed, "What can I learn to live with?"

Blair moved from Pennsylvania to a desert community near Albuquerque: "There are no green trees here. It's all desert! I can't change the climate. I miss watching the seasons change, even raking leaves in the fall. I can visit the state park to learn more about this landscape so I can see its unique richness. I can also schedule a weekend away this fall, to see the leaves again. But it won't be the same."

Leslie misses the quiet of her former country home: "I have lost the view of the lake that I had before. I used to get up early to go for a walk and listen to the birds. Now I am near a small park. Every night I hear sirens and horns and automated bus stop announcements. It's like something out of a science fiction movie."

Blair may learn to love the desert, but Leslie probably will not be happy as long as she lives in the city. Her values conflict with what she sees and hears.

Taking Charge of Your Resistance

Many people will tell you seriously, "You won't find happiness in a new place until you make peace with your present demons." When people relax and stop fighting, their minds can move to a constructive, problem-solving mode. The following exercises offer some approaches to help you understand and deal with your resistance.

== **Exercise** ===
Pockets of Joy

Every day, try to find at least one small moment that makes you glad to be alive.

• Did you notice beauty around you—a sunset or a sunrise, palm trees or pine trees, a neighbor's garden?

- Did anyone offer a friendly gesture—a friendly smile, a compliment, even a hug?

- Did you do something you liked: baked a cake, read the perfect murder mystery, tended a garden, shopped the local mall, lifted weights at the gym?

- Did you hear from an old friend or relative?

It's easy to overlook these small moments when you are unhappy. But if you seek them out, you may find yourself feeling happier and stronger, even if you still want to move again.

Exercise
Visualize Leaving

Most resisters love doing this one!

Every day when you wake up, write down a detailed description of where you'd like to be. Use a notebook, a scratch pad, or even a computer file. Write a detailed description of your ideal location as if you were living there now. Use present tense.

> *I am now living in a beautiful house in the southwestern U.S. I am back in the desert, enjoying the fantastic sunsets, riding horses on weekends. I earn a comfortable living that can easily support the lifestyle. Every morning I take the two dogs for a walk, enjoying the outdoors . . .*

Continue as long as you like. After you've finished writing, put the paper away (or close the computer file) and focus on the present. Change will happen.

Exercise
The Obstacle Course

If you've determined you can't make your new location work, you need to find out what is holding you back from moving. Sometimes you can change your reality.

List obstacles to the move. Job? Family pressures? Commitments to mortgage or car?

List costs to remove. What would it cost to remove this obstacle? Don't just say, "Too much!" Imagine that you had just won the Super Lottery and money is no object.

For instance, perhaps you moved to Arizona to be near an aging parent. You love your family and want to spend more time with them, but you really can't adjust to hundred-degree summers and dry, warm winters. You need to ask yourself what it would cost to fly to Arizona on weekends from your desired destination, or to fly your parent to your new destination for visits. Can you substitute phone calls for visits? How about e-mail?

Edgar had a revelation after he moved to Florida to be near his wife's parents. These kinfolk had always seemed delighted to see their children and grandchildren. Sometimes they even seemed dependent on the "young folks" for a social life. Yet one day the older couple admitted they could use more time for themselves. "A little too much togetherness," his father-in-law said.

Harriet transferred to Minneapolis because her promotion required her to work at the company headquarters. After two years, she was supposed to transfer back to Dallas, but the company restructured. Now, they told her, her future lay in Minnesota. Harriet found the winters unbearable and the people were . . . well, different from those in Texas.

Although her field offered fewer opportunities in Texas, Harriet began job-hunting at once. She took a twenty percent pay cut in order to move back to Dallas. Her risk paid off. Because she was now more comfortable, she was more effective with clients and colleagues. As a result, she was promoted to new responsibilities and was soon earning more than she had before. Harriet is happier today than she was before the move to Minneapolis. "I know what I have," she says, "and what I almost lost."

Moving Tip
Keep an Eye on the Movers

If you hire professional movers, photograph the items you value most highly, whether their value is sentimental or monetary. Take photos as the packers begin so you can establish that your items were undamaged before they were loaded. Then take photos of these items as they are unloaded, preferably with the drivers standing next to them. Also as you open boxes, photograph those that were packed improperly, such as a fragile item packed without paper wrapping. These photos will come in handy when complaining to an unsatisfactory moving company.

If your packers do not seem to be doing a good, careful job, call the dispatcher immediately to report the problem. The company may send out a supervisor or a new team. If not, make a note of the situation immediately to document your concerns. If you've already packed away the computer, a handwritten note will be just fine. Save all your damaged items until they're inspected. Keep receipts for repairs. Your renter's or homeowner's insurance may cover losses due to fire and theft, but rarely do they cover losses due to bad movers. If you encounter problems, I recommend calling the head office of the moving company rather than the local agent. In my experience they are more responsive to complaints.

10

"We're More Than the Sum of Our Identities"

The Family Move

Because jobs were scarce in Howard's field, Joan and Howard found themselves in a medium-sized, Midwestern city. They loved the lifestyle, their children joined the hockey team, and they realized all their needs could be met—except one. Joan, an elementary school teacher, could not get a job in the area. There was a waiting list for positions at every school in a hundred-mile radius. They bought a nice house and began to make friends, but they missed Joan's income and Joan really missed working. The couple explored alternatives. Could Joan commute to a job? Could she start a business working out of her new home? Would she want to use this time to go back to school?

Changing the Family Identity

When you move as a family, you are negotiating two levels of identity simultaneously: your own identity as "John" or "Jane" and your contribution to the identity of "The Doe Family." The family identity undergoes a transformation parallel to the individual's.

The Family Self-Concept

Families, like individuals, can find their identities being challenged. While they lived in a small town in Vermont, the Harrisons had gained a local reputation as athletes. "All the Harrisons play basketball," was the way they would be introduced. All four children, boys and girls, starred on school teams from sixth grade through high school. Bill, the father, coached one son's teams and Jean, the mother, attended every game.

Unexpectedly, the family had to move when Bill's business was bought out by a competitor. "I'm too young to retire," said Bill, "and with four kids going to college, I need to keep working." Bill became a consultant in a larger Midwestern city.

The family liked the new city, and the children were excited to try out for basketball teams. Ed, the second son, was crushed when he didn't make junior varsity. "It's more competitive here," he shrugged. Bill did not feel ready to begin coaching again. Now when people said "the Harrisons," it was "the new family." In their new city, the family members were meeting people one at a time. Their identity as a family would take time to grow. "When I sign a check in the supermarket," Jean said, "the cashier doesn't ask if I'm related to that kid who won the game for the high school. We're just not known as a family."

═══ Exercise ═══
Your Family Name

It's helpful if you get clear on how things may change when you move. Think about the following questions and how your family self-concept may change.

• In your current residence (or in your previous residence, if you've already moved), how is your family known in the community?

• Do you have a family identity? and if so, how are you described?

For example:

The Smiths who live in that big house.

The Ryersons who always have people over at Christmas.

• How do you think your identity will change after you move?

For example:

We'll be the new people who bought the old Grayson place.
We won't know anybody so we won't be known for parties for a
while.

"We're Not the Same Family"

The family self-concept often changes after a move. Roles and dynamics within the family can be transformed unexpectedly as each family member responds to the new environment in a different way. Tom, a high school football coach, moved to Wyoming because he loved the outdoors. He became involved in camping, fishing, and hunting, even flying a small airplane. His wife, also a high school teacher, soon realized she hated the cold and the outdoor life. She particularly hated flying, which was becoming Tom's passion. Soon the couple was talking about separation. She wanted "civilization" and he wouldn't give up his new life.

Your Family Social Identity

While each member of a family negotiates a new social identity, family units also develop a relationship with their new community. When you've lived in a place for a long time, you don't have to explain what you do. "We keep Wednesday night as Family Night." "We take turns cooking on week nights." When you move, your new neighbors may have established different family patterns and may find your style a little unnerving.

June and Ben wanted a very close family and always agreed that they would not go out during the week in order to stay home with the children. After they moved, Ben found his new colleagues liked to go out together for a drink after work a couple of nights a week. His new company was more conservative and he found he was the only man who shared responsibility for cooking and cleaning at home. Nobody said anything, but "Ben felt there was an unspoken question: 'What kind of family do you have?'"

Children, especially teenagers, can report problems adjusting to a new social world if family rules are too strict—"Nobody here has to be home by ten. They think my family must be a prison"—or too lenient—"No curfew? They think I'm wild!" It may take some time before you feel your neighbors have accepted your differences.

Your Family Paper Identity

Because so much of your paper identity depends on your job, the spouse who moves without a job may feel a loss of self. This can create stress for both people as they try to negotiate what seems like an unfair situation. Some families deal with this by designing relocation into their career choices. One partner can develop a mobile career, such as freelance writing or computer consulting, so that if a spouse has to move, they can easily continue their jobs.

Of course, what constitutes a mobile career will vary over time. In the United States of the fifties and sixties, a spouse could easily obtain employment as a librarian, schoolteacher, or social worker. Now those jobs tend to be highly prized, sometimes unionized, with a long waiting list. Temporary secretarial work no longer is available for the asking. Teachers find jobs scarce as they accumulate experience. "My sister's husband got me this job," says Olga, a third-grade teacher. "If he hadn't been in the district, nobody would have looked at my résumé." For several years, Gregory, a CPA, found that he could change jobs when his partner, Tom, moved for a promotion. However, he says, "I can't do this forever. So far we've been lucky."

When both partners choose fields where jobs are scarce, a long-distance marriage may change the entire definition of the family. Helen teaches Medieval French literature, while her husband Leonard specializes in Near Eastern studies. "I haven't been able to find one university where we can both work," she says. Kaylene, a third-grade teacher, chose to remain in Jacksonville when her husband moved to Tennessee for a better job. "Our last child went to college, and my husband works all the time anyway," Kaylene says. "My husband doesn't make friends as easily as I do so he's lonelier than I am. Things are going to be tough for a while."

When a family cannot move as a unit, identity changes become considerably more complex. If you face this decision, you will probably need to turn to specialized resources for guidance. Complexities of those family situations extend beyond relocation.

Who's Moving and Who's Being Moved?

When a family moves, the members are divided into "who moves" and "who is moved." The person who originates the move tends to be happier than the person who's along for the ride. This pattern has been reported in one study after another and researchers have reached a consensus: a major source of family stress is the failure of one partner to find a job

Traditionally, the mover is the husband while the person being moved is the wife, but more and more the reverse holds true. One woman I interviewed turned down an academic job because there were no opportunities for her husband, a computer salesperson, to work in his field. Another man I spoke with made it easy for him to move with his wife by starting a home-based business.

Adaskin (1987) studied fifty-three families who moved within North America. All moved to follow the husband's job. Adaskin found that wives and teenage children reported the greatest degree of anger. This anger seemed to come from feelings of helplessness. Their anger turned to resentment against the family member who initiated the move and ultimately the whole experience of moving.

Adaskin's study found that husbands and wives ranked the severity of their sources of stress differently. These differences do not seem to be related to career roles, as most wives in the study were college-educated, and less than half (42 percent) stayed home. Wives included "missing old friends" and "making new friends" in the top three, while husbands placed greater importance on "finding a home" and "financial worries."

Because their concerns differ, family members may have difficulty appreciating each other's needs during a move. When one partner follows another, the one leading may view the move as "a great career opportunity," while the one following views the same move as "a need to make new friends."

For the trailing spouse, it can be difficult to admit, "I dread moving and I resent the fact that I have to pull up roots because of my partner's needs." Yet these feelings often arise from genuine hardship.

═══ Exercise ═══
What's in It for Me?

In order to clarify your feelings about this move and its effects on your family, answer the following questions. Have each member of your family do the same.

- How will you benefit from this move?

- How do you believe your partner will benefit from this move?

- How do you believe your children will benefit from this move?

- What, if anything, do you feel you are giving up for this move?

- What do you dread most about this move?

If you are still in the decision-making stage, you may want to encourage your partner to complete this exercise also. If one partner strongly resents the move, you may want to explore alternative options.

If you have committed to the move, you can use this exercise to identify aspects of your destination that need to be researched. Use the exercises in chapter 2 to learn more about your destination.

If you absolutely must move and you find yourself feeling extremely resentful, you need to acknowledge your feelings before you move. Sometimes simply acknowledging your feelings will defuse your anger. You may decide to talk to a professional counselor. There are no simple answers. Some people have left a marriage or relationship rather than move again. Others feel committed to follow "whither thou goest."

Should You Hold a Family Meeting on Moving?

Deirdre, along with her husband and three children, made a high-risk move from Denver to Seattle to be closer to Deirdre's family. "Timothy and I decided we wanted to move," she said. "We weighed the trade-offs. I was more positive about the move because I had family and I knew my secretarial skills could go anywhere. We had many discussions and weighed all the trade-offs. We didn't talk to the children until we had made the decision to move.

"Let's face it," Deirdre continued, "we're the adults. We know our kids. If one kid would be seriously harmed by the move, we'd know. We know who's in the last year of junior high and who has a once-in-a-lifetime opportunity to play on a championship team. We make the decisions and the children have to accept them. It's good for them to learn that we don't always get what we want."

Eileen and Ralph chose a different approach. "Our kids were in high school when we began to think about changing our lifestyle and moving to the country. We told them what we were thinking and asked for their input. We made it clear, though, that we'd make the final decision."

When I talked to people about family moves, they agreed on one point: Don't ask for advice or hold a family meeting unless you are really going to listen to your children. Don't hold a vote if you're prepared to exercise veto power.

Choosing Who Does What

Family roles often change during a move. "Helen was always the take-charge person," says Bruce, "but when we moved, she got called away to take care of her mother's illness. I had to do everything." "My husband was never there," says Roxanne, who is now divorced. "I was the one who dealt with the moving company. Husbands won't step into an argument with other men."

Dividing up the duties can be a great way to get everyone involved and to take advantage of each person's strengths. Lillian and Julie found they brought different skills to the move. "Lillian could negotiate with the moving company," says Julie, "but I could get us organized at the other end. I arranged the furniture and put the bookshelves together while Lillian went off to get her job started."

When family members have resistance to a move, you will have difficulty gaining cooperation. People will resist accepting any roles associated with moving. It's important to recognize that their resistance is valid, but you also need to emphasize that moving is a family project and that everyone needs to pitch in. "We had to move when I was a little girl," Karlene says. "I hated leaving our house. I loved my room and my neighborhood. My mother was great; every time I'd feel sad she'd give me a quick hug and say something about how tough it was and ask me how I was feeling. But then she'd turn the conversation to moving and we'd talk about what I could do to help. She got me to focus on how happy I was now. She made the chores fun. I inventoried my clothes and toys and packed them up myself. She kept me busy the entire time. It worked! I began to feel like it was part of an adventure."

Once you are committed to moving, make a list of what needs to be done. Decide ahead of time what each family member's role will be. Remember when things don't go as planned to be flexible. "I thought I could deal with the utility hook-ups," says Vernon, "but I got called out of town on an emergency from work." "I promised to inspect everything coming off the truck," says Anne, "but I was too exhausted. I should have asked one of the children to help."

Begin by finding out what each family member wants to do. Everyone can help with packing. Older children can be stationed in various rooms of a house to direct the moving company, or they can help take inventory as items come off the truck, calling an adult to verify damages. They can also call for food when you're faced with feeding a hungry family in an empty house. Nobody knows more about ordering pizza than a college student home from school!

=== Exercise ===
Who Does What?

When dividing up the moving chores, it's important to find out who wants to do what. By giving your family some feeling of control over their work, you'll find your helpers are more cooperative.

What does each family member want to contribute?

Name	Activity
_____	_____
_____	_____
_____	_____
_____	_____

Now, make a list of what everyone does NOT want to do. Some family members will be hopeless at certain tasks. Others simply hate doing them. If you identify a chore that nobody wants to do, you may want to offer a special reward or treat for whoever takes on whatever your family considers the most odious chore. Or you may decide to give everyone a treat by hiring outside help.

What does each family member NOT want to contribute?

Name	Activity
_____	_____
_____	_____
_____	_____
_____	_____

Talking with Your Teenager

Researchers and counselors agree: You can anticipate the greatest resistance about moving from your teenagers, and for good reason.

Teenagers are particularly vulnerable to social influence and they want to be accepted by their peers. Because they value these attachments so highly, they will be resistant to breaking the attachments they've made and starting up new attachment in your new location. If their new group withholds acceptance, the teen's self-concept will be threatened. An adult might be able to dismiss a group's prejudices by saying, "I know who I am," but teenagers, who are still developing their self-concepts, depend a great deal more on the group to validate their identities.

Acknowledge the Pressure They Are Feeling

Acceptance typically is based on conformity, on being "like the rest of us," and "fitting in." A teenager who moves to a new location often does not look or talk or feel like his or her new classmates. Harry, raised on the Florida coast, met his new classmates in Tennessee and was discouraged: "It's only September and they've lost their tans!"

Some adults retain vivid memories of a teenage relocation for their entire lives. Although Arlene, aged thirty-two, has established a successful career and a happy marriage, her voice still shakes as she recalls her family's move from Pittsburgh to Minneapolis: "I had just finished my sophomore year of high school. I was starting to feel accepted for the first time. I was a cheerleader. I had a boyfriend and a date to the prom. Suddenly I was in a whole new world. Their culture was different. Their clothing was different. Their music was different.

"They hated me," Arlene continues, as if she were talking about an event that happened yesterday. "I talked about Pittsburgh, where I'd lived all my life, but no one in Minneapolis had any interest in Pittsburgh. They wanted to talk local gossip and I didn't know any."

Arlene's life was changed permanently by her experience. She started her own business so she would never be at the mercy of a corporate mandate to move: "I will never, ever leave this city," she says firmly and most of her friends believe her.

At thirty-five, Harriet still feels uneasy about her family's frequent moves due to her father's military career. She sometimes feels bitter at the missed opportunities. Harriet's dancing lessons were interrupted: "I took up figure skating, but it wasn't the same." Harriet still remembers spending her senior year of high school adjusting to new faces: "I felt like a nerd. It was awful." And, she says today, "I've done well and I have a good career. But I'm still a little shy, and I still feel like I've missed out."

Be Sensitive to Their Needs

Many parents respect their children's needs, often adjusting the timing of a move to allow children to finish high school in one location. Mary, a single parent, turned down a promotion so that she wouldn't uproot her ninth-grade son, who played on an elite hockey team, coached by a famous professional who played for her city's team. Her son idolized the coach and the team was his life.

Herb's family had no choice. Herb's father worked for a major corporation that, in those days, moved managers every three years. Herb had just completed three years of high school when the cycle began again. This time Herb arranged to stay behind, spending a year with the family of his best friend. Herb remains grateful that he could finish his high school career with his friends. The year spent away from his family did not affect his closeness with his own parents and his sister, who was just starting junior high when they moved.

Other parents, and sometimes the teens themselves, opt for creative solutions during a move. Fred and Nanette had joint custody of Michael, who was fourteen when they divorced. Fred stayed in Arizona while Nanette moved to Texas. Michael asked his parents to send him to boarding school in Colorado, so he would have some stability during the school year and remain on neutral ground. Michael is now attending college, living in a dormitory, and the family reports satisfaction with the arrangement.

Understand That Teenagers May See Moving as an Escape

What if your teen is miserable now? At fourteen, Danielle was going through a tough time. She was overweight, her math teacher had taken a dislike to her, and her shyness kept her from making new friends. When Danielle's father was transferred unexpectedly, Danielle began to fantasize. "After we move, I'll be thinner and I'll have new friends. The kids in Maplewood won't be mean like the kids here." Danielle's mother tried to be realistic, saying, "Try to find something good here and now. You might like Maplewood better, but you'll still have to take algebra."

Sometimes children *do* escape. Danielle might lose weight over the summer or she might find a new best friend in her new class. If your son has acquired a reputation for being different or "weird," he may be able to start fresh in his new school. If your daughter is just beginning high school, she can indeed escape whatever reputation she built up with the children she knew in grade school.

Joel was thrilled when his family moved just before his sophomore year of high school. "My brother Paul was two years ahead of me, all through school," he remembers. "When we moved, he stayed behind to finish his senior year. I was finally out of his shadow. If we hadn't moved, I'd have always been Paul's little brother. Paul played varsity baseball and ran track. The gym teacher would have expected me to try out for those teams, but I hated that stuff. At my new school, I ended up editing the school paper and playing trumpet in the marching band. And now that we're both out of school, Paul and I are very close."

Talking with Your Younger Children

Having young children can actually help parents adjust to a new community. Attending PTA meetings and sports events are great ways to meet other parents. Olive, a single parent of a nine-year-old daughter, moved to a Midwestern city. Her daughter became involved in softball and Girl Scouts, and Olive soon met the parents of her daughter's friends.

Parents who are interviewed about moving always express surprise at the resilience of their young children. But a study by Amiram Raviv and his colleagues (1990) found that children were definitely stressed by moving. While adults report moving as twenty-eighth of forty-three stressful life events, a ninth-grade group rated moving seventh out of thirty-seven. Pre-adolescents (aged ten to thirteen) reported greater stress than adolescents (aged fourteen to eighteen), particularly social stress. The researchers suggest that older adolescents may have more resources to help them deal with loss, such as the ability to maintain contact with former friends.

Get Children Involved in Planning

In the same study of adolescent reactions to a household move (Raviv et al. 1990), researchers asked children what factors contributed to easing the stress. Children said they appreciated support from family and friends, as well as encouragement from older siblings. However, the most important factor was the degree to which they could participate in planning the move. The people I interviewed for this study offered similar advice.

Discuss the Move with Children

Buy or borrow books and videotapes about moving and about your new location. Try to schedule a visit with the children. Plan family meetings to discuss practical details, and also emotions. Sometimes children will have fears that seem bizarre to adults. "One of my kids thought we'd leave him behind," says Iris. "The other one thought our old home would disappear after we left."

Bill hasn't gotten over his family's style of moving: "We moved three times before I started high school. Each time, the kids would go off to school in the morning, and while we were gone, our parents would pack up the house and the movers would come. We'd come home to an empty house and right away we'd drive to the new one." Bill and his sisters still find these memories upsetting. "There was no chance to say good-bye, and we really wanted to pack our own stuff."

Bill encourages his own children to feel involved in the whole process, even in the house-hunting decision. "They know the parents will make the final decision," he says, "but we use their input." When children say, "We hate this house," you can say, "Let's talk about why you hate it. What can we do to fix things?"

"You can begin to teach your children about making trade-offs," says Connie, who recently moved with her husband and two pre-teens. "This house doesn't have a porch, but it does have a big yard."

Keep Everybody Busy

Timing is critical. Children who enter school right away will adjust faster. "We moved in August and school didn't start until September fourteenth. The neighbors had all taken their kids and gone to the shore. It was awful. We were busy settling in and our children had nothing to do all day."

Avoid Being Over-Protective

Making friends is a skill that requires learning. "When Jamie came in crying, my heart went out to her," says Sylvia. "She said nobody liked her at school. I told her that some things just take time. She had always made friends easily so I knew it was just a matter of time. I absolutely did not get involved and now Jamie's just fine."

Visit Your Child's School

You can learn quickly if a child has problems, if you get involved in the child's school. Often it takes a while to learn the subtle nuances of classroom dynamics, reward/punishment systems, and holiday customs that may be different. When Frank brought his child to school, he explained to the principal, "My son will be taking off all the Jewish holidays in September." Learning that few Jewish children were enrolled in this elementary school, he offered to make a presentation to his son's class to explain their customs.

Be a Positive Influence

Even if you are deeply unhappy with your new community, encourage your child to appreciate its positive qualities. If you feel so strongly about it that you need to disparage most of the local customs and values, you should seriously consider moving, sending your child to boarding school, and/or getting the best counseling you can afford. A child should not be encouraged to feel alienated from his or her environment. Your attitude is contagious: your misery becomes theirs.

"We moved to a small town in Michigan when I was just starting school," recalls David. "My parents were New Yorkers and they hated every moment of the move. My father loved his job, but he made fun of everything and everybody in town. My mother managed to insult everybody we met by reminding them how superior New York was. The local kids kept telling me to get out of town and move back East.

"As an adult," David says, "I have to be careful not to do the same thing. When I moved to St. Louis from Boston, I found myself criticizing everything in sight, although there's really a lot of good stuff to do in St. Louis. Now I'm moving to Cleveland, Ohio, and I am determined to be totally positive, if only for the kids."

Help Your Children Maintain a Continuous Sense of Identity

Children, especially younger children, often feel that their world has disintegrated after they move. A familiar home gives a child an important sense of security.

Take Children's Fantasies Seriously

Some children develop fantasies about the destruction of their worlds. "When we moved to St. Louis," says David, "we took the children back to Boston. One of the children was very happy to see her old house was still standing. I was afraid she'd want to move back, but she didn't. She was just afraid her old neighborhood had disappeared."

Be Aware That Children Become Attached to Possessions

"When we moved," says Louise, "I decorated their new rooms to look just like the ones we left behind. I think the children really appreciated waking up to a familiar room." Of course, Louise realized, her children were young; older children would want to plan their own rooms.

Each Family Member's Response Is Unique

While researchers and counselors tend to focus on differences based on age and sex, the adjustment to a move will also be influenced by personality and social differences. Vincent, who I interviewed for this book, reflected on his family's move from Wisconsin to Iowa:

"Travis had friends in Wisconsin but he is not a very social person. He doesn't need to have friends around. He is perfectly content to read a book or draw or listen to music. He knew a lot of people from school, but didn't socialize as much as our other son does. Our younger son, Wayne, is a social butterfly. He had tons of really close friends in Wisconsin. He needs to be around a lot of people and he's always on the go. Before we moved we really worried about Wayne because he had all of these close friends.

"It turns out that the transition was very easy for Wayne and very difficult for Travis. Wayne just made new friends, in an amazingly short time. He kept in touch with his old friends but less so as time has gone on. Wayne's social anchor is close friends which he replaced. Travis's social anchor wasn't individuals but context. Travis felt that he belonged to groups in Wisconsin. He identified with school and with his hockey team, even though most of the kids weren't close friends. I think even the city itself was Travis's anchor; the misses the entertainment section of the paper.

Frank's sons had different styles of relating to the places they lived. These differences have been described by sociologist Robert Weiss (1990, 4) as relationships of attachment and relationships of community. Relationships of attachment involve bonding with particular friends in order to reinforce a continuing sense of self. Relationships of community offer a sense of place and a feeling of identifying with a larger group. Some children, and some adults, emphasize one aspect of identity more than the other.

======= **Moving Tip** =======

Create a Service Team

As you get settled in your new community, you can create a team of service support people. Often good service people know one another. The glass company that replaced your broken window may recommend a carpenter to fix the molding. Your pet sitter may know a lawn care service. After all, many of these people live in the area and many own their own homes. However, you should always get references from current customers.

As a newcomer, be cautious when choosing services from the telephone book or the Internet. Try to obtain references before signing a contract, spending large sums of money, or hiring for high-risk repairs. If you don't know anyone to ask, make a personal visit to learn about prices and service options. I've asked people in the parking lot, "How long have you been coming here? What's your experience?" If they're very happy or very unhappy, they'll be delighted to share their views. I found a great mechanic by asking a stranger whose older car appeared to be lovingly maintained.

11

"Moving Alone Is Like One Hand Clapping"

The Solo Move

When Lillian moved to a suburb of Minneapolis, five years ago, she faced some of the challenges of moving alone. "I chose a beautiful house," she says. "I'd just gotten a big promotion and I wanted to splurge. The house was on a quiet cul-de-sac, with only seven other homes. The day the moving company delivered my furniture, I was feeling thoroughly frazzled. So I was delighted when five women from the neighborhood came over to say hello. They brought all kinds of homemade goodies: pastry, cake, donuts, cookies; there must have been a pile a foot high on the coffee table. We all sat down on chairs that still had moving stickers on them and they welcomed me to the neighborhood. Then somebody asked, 'Where's your husband? What does he do?' 'I don't have a husband,' I said. 'There's just me. I have a son from my first marriage but he lives in Alabama." Suddenly the women looked at each other. They all got up, said hasty good-byes, and walked out. I've never seen people move so fast in my life."

At the time, Lillian recalls, "I was so hurt. What did I do to offend them? I wasn't after their husbands. I had a boyfriend of my own. What did they think would happen?" Eventually, Lillian said, they got to know each other. She knew she was accepted, she says, when they invited her to a Super Bowl party after she'd been there just over a year.

Moving to the suburb challenged Lillian's self-concept as a single, professional woman. Yet in this neighborhood, newcomers were defined by their marital status, not their professional roles. "My neighbors had no idea who I was or what I did with my life," she says now. "I was threatened by them but they were even more threatened by me. To them, I was a sophisticated career woman from New York. I traveled all over the United States. I had meetings just like their husbands did. I needed to reassure them. But at the time, all I could think was, 'My God, I've just moved here and they hate me!'"

Unique Challenges for the Solo Mover

Studies of relocation rarely discuss concerns of those who move by themselves. In his studies of corporate relocation, Munton (1993) briefly mentions a professional woman who depended a great deal on her mother. If you move alone, without the benefit of supportive parents with time on their hands, you may find little help during a difficult transition. Unlike those who move as a family and have to balance potentially conflicting interests of the family members, the solo mover has to balance personal and business demands, which often translates to giving up social networks to accommodate the demands of a job. Being single—never-married, divorced, or widowed—poses special challenges for the following reasons.

It Can Be Hard to Fit In

Many locales are set up for the married person with two kids and a station wagon. "Can you believe this?" exclaimed Suzanne. "The dry cleaners all closed at six o'clock during the week. I'm an accountant. How am I supposed to drop off my clothes during tax season? There's only one other single woman in town and she lives with her mother. Everybody else is married."

Other times, single people do not have access to the idyllic charm of small town living. Melba moved to a small Midwestern town to accept an administrative position in the local college. "I liked the idea of living in a small town." she says, "I thought I'd be part of a tight-knit community, where people feel close to one another. Yet I feel very isolated here. It's just hard to be single when lives revolve around soccer games, swim meets, and other stuff the kids do. If you're not involved with kids, you're not involved with anything.

"If I were a parent," Melba continues, "my priorities would probably be different. I'd be getting the kids involved in Little League games and dance lessons, and with my job, that would take all the energy I have."

These Rules Were Written for Someone Else's Game

Many companies allow managerial employees time to help their family and children get settled, but expect single employees to begin work right away. Those who move on their own express enormous resentment for these policies, which may be part of the informal culture or written in a company manual.

Somebody has to be home when people come to install cable, telephone, and other services. If you're single, that somebody will be you. "Who's supposed to sit there and wait for the utility hook-ups"? wonders Jeff, who moved shortly after his divorce. "Perhaps I should train the dog to let them in."

You may need to make extra trips to the dry cleaner, hardware store, or repair shop right after you move. Few adults can avoid a visit to the Department of Motor Vehicles. You may find yourself spending hours on the phone with the moving company to discuss the damage they did to your possessions. You cannot delegate these chores to a spouse or child and you probably haven't made close friends in the new city. Your employer may be surprised when you take time off for these settling-in chores.

When the rules seem to ignore your needs, your identity can become problematic. "I have to keep asking for exceptions to regular company policies," says Margaret. "I missed an important event because the moving company showed up at the same time. People thought I was weird because I didn't have someone to help me. It bothers me to feel like I don't fit in."

In some cities, you can find services to help you deal with these time pressures. You may be able to hire someone to stand in line at the motor vehicles bureau (they'll register the car but you still have to pass the driving test), wait for the plumber, or take your cat to the vet. Look in the Yellow Pages under Shopping Services—Personal. Often these companies have the word "errands" in their names. A number of pet-sitting services will pick up your pet, keep your vet appointment, and return the animal to your home. In fact, if you are looking for a pet-sitter, ask your veterinarian. Sometimes veterinary technicians will be moonlighting—and they know how to give a pill to a cat.

Richard learned to be creative: "I hired the teenagers in my neighborhood. The fourteen-year-old next door would walk the dog and shovel snow. The sixteen-year-old could pick up cleaning and run errands—all for a fee, of course. I talked to the parents first, and we agreed on how much the kids could work and what would be a fair wage. The parents didn't want me paying too much or letting the kids get away with sloppy work."

Help Can Be Hard to Find

Henrietta had just moved to a small town in Oklahoma. "Being sick in a new town, where I didn't know anybody, was kind of scary. I don't mind saying I was feeling kind of sorry for myself. I ended up having to go to the emergency room at one A.M. and I had to drive myself in my car." The experience, Henrietta says, "kind of delineated who my friends were; who said, 'call me next time,' not just 'sorry to hear that.' You want someone there to hold your hand and tell you you're gonna feel better."

Jim had just moved to a new house without a phone when his car battery died. "You need friends and they need to be there," he says now. "Long-distance calls are fine but sometimes you just need another person nearby who can lend you a hand. If there's a couple, one can stay with the luggage and one can go get help. It's as simple as that."

Business Travel Can Be Destructive

While a married person's spouse can maintain some activity when the partner goes out of town, the single person's social network gets completely disrupted during an absence.

Lillian, the woman whose neighbors welcomed her to Minneapolis with pastries, says her difficulties were exacerbated by frequent business travel. "I missed the neighborhood garage sales and the weekend barbecues. I missed Halloween, when I might have gotten to know the kids. When I was out of town I lost all continuity."

"Sometimes I don't bother coming home at all," says Hal. "If I'm going to Houston on business, I'll just hang out there and catch a movie or a game. Why go home? I don't know anybody, and, at this rate, I'm not going to."

Holidays Can Be Brutal

"I don't want to go to the boss's house for dinner," says Jim. "If I don't have friends and can't get home to the family, I'll spend Thanksgiving in front of the tube, with pizza and beer and a lot of long-distance calls." "I stayed home and cried," Marilyn says of her first Thanksgiving in a new home. "To this day, I can't understand why nobody called or invited me over. It was as though I didn't exist."

Theresa disagrees. "I'd rather be alone than spend holidays with strangers," she says. "I'm not a waif or a stray. I'd rather do something I enjoy. Last time I got invited to dinner I ended up as a referee in a family fight. Who needs it?" Theresa has come up with a method for turning down unwanted invitations: "I've learned to be less than truthful. I never say, 'No thank you, I'd rather be alone.' I say, 'I'm spending the holidays with friends or family.' Otherwise they hassle me."

═ Exercise ═
Living Alone

If you are moving as a single person, whether you are divorced, widowed, or never-married, you need to get clear on what problems you may face when you move.

What challenges do you anticipate in your new location? Will you miss family or friends? Will it be difficult to find a new life while keeping up with the demands of work? Will you need some free time before you can meet people? Will you be the only single man or woman in town?

List the obstacles you think you might face when you move.

_____

_____

_____

Think about what aspect of your identity will be affected by each obstacle.
For instance,

I expect to be the only single woman at company social events. Both my social and paper identity will be affected. They'll view me as weird, and my position in the company can be challenged.

Keep this list handy as you read through the rest of the chapter.

Self-Concept Challenges

Being alone forces you to ask question, "Who am I?" Many people's conceptions of themselves as healthy and happy are related to their connections to others. Helga says, "If you have family you have automatic connections. If you have connections, you're happier. Feeling unconnected is difficult. Nobody's depending on me! People help me create meaning in my life. I need something to push me, motivate me, make me want to get out of bed. What do you do when you're tired of having dinner for the fifth night in a row by yourself?"

"I Can't Do Things That Are the Real Me"

While many single people take pride in their homes, others find activities outside the home as the primary means to express their self-concept. These activities can range from participating in sports to painting watercolors to going to the movies.

Even solitary activities at home may be affected by a move, as the new home may not be conducive to certain types of activity. "Back home in Connecticut," mourns Virginia, "I had a beautiful sunroom where I kept my plants. I loved to sit and embroider, looking out of the window. Now I am living in this boring apartment. I can't find a place where I enjoy just sitting quietly, so I find myself watching television or going to the mall more often."

"The mood here is different," says Walter, who had moved to Florida from Philadelphia. "Back home, there was a lot of culture. Here the motto is, 'Life is a beach.' Well, it's fun to play, but I miss the intellectual conversations. In Philadelphia, you could meet interesting people on the train, in the coffee shop—anywhere. Here we sit in our cars and talk to our neighbors."

"Why Am I Doing This?"

The challenge of a move can be so great that people forget why they embarked on their adventure in the first place. "I knew I needed three years of experience with a production group," says Richard. "I really didn't want to move to a small city in Illinois, but the opportunity was there at the time I needed it for my career. When I first moved, I got really frustrated with the place: nobody to talk to, no place to go, not even a decent movie theater. I loved the job, but socially I was dying. Then one day an ex-girlfriend called to chat, and she reminded me why I had moved. I didn't come for the social life and I wasn't going to get much. So I focused on work and carved out as much time as possible to spend weekends in Chicago and St. Louis, where I could get culture and friends and still be me. I used the time alone to build my skills at work and, for fun, started distance running."

"I had just gotten laid off for the third time in four years," says Alice, a computer graphics specialist. "This was the only job I could get. I hate the place and I want to make sure I don't ever have to do this again. I'm not crazy about the job, but I do have time to do some freelance work and build up my skills on somebody else's payroll. The town? Forget it. If I make friends, fine. If not—well, phone rates have come down a lot, and I can always go home for the holidays and long weekends."

Thelma was happy but lonely. "I've sacrificed my personal life to my career for ten years," she said. "I've lived in places where I felt like an alien, although my career really took off. Now I'm finally living in a place I like, but I don't know a soul. I don't know where to get started. And what happens if I meet people and have to move again? I'll have another round of good-byes and go back to being lonely in a new city. So I stay late at the office and work even harder—and run up a big long-distance bill talking to my family and my old college roommate."

Richard, Alice, and Thelma have different approaches to their new lives. Richard will focus on his work with his employer, hoping to build his résumé and move within the company. His priorities lie with his job. He will probably socialize a great deal with his co-workers, hoping to make contacts for his future.

Alice needs to carve out time for her own work. Her evenings and weekends will be spent building her portfolio and she may take courses or study independently to build her skills. Her priorities involve seeking solitude and unstructured time away from her job. While she will be free from the distraction of a social network, she may find herself growing lonely, especially if she works at home for long periods of time.

Thelma will be least concerned with her career. She may even sacrifice salary or promotions in order to live in a place where she feels comfortable. Her priorities include seeking out ways to remain in the location she loves. What will she do if her company downsizes? Perhaps she can start a business. At the same time, she needs to make friends and build a long-term support network.

═ Exercise
Why Am I Here?

When you identify your priorities you might discover what you need to do to make your new location work for you. Fill out this worksheet and spend some time considering what it is that you want most.

I moved here because _____

Now what I need most is _____

Three of my goals for the next six months are . . .

_____

_____

_____

To achieve those goals, I need to spend MORE time . . .

_____

_____

_____

I need to spend LESS time . . .

_____

_____

_____

I anticipate that a year from now I will need . . .

_____

_____

_____

To meet those needs, I have to start . . .

_____

_____

_____

I plan to stay here for _____ years (months) because . . .

_____

_____

_____

Thelma wrote:

I moved here because I got a big promotion and a raise. A great career move.

Now what I need most is someone to talk to when I get home. I'm beginning to wish I didn't have to move again.

Three of my goals for the next six months are (1) network and meet new people, (2) see if there's a way to put down roots so I won't have to move again, and (3) keep my career going.

To achieve these goals, I need to spend MORE time joining groups outside my company and LESS time working at night on the laptop.

I anticipate that a year from now I will need friends and a personal life.

To meet those needs, I have to find time to let people into my life.

I plan to stay here for three years because they'll move me again.

Thelma stopped when she'd gotten this far. She realized she did not like this answer. Instead, she wanted to stay in her new city. She loved the museums, the shops, and the parks. "I could take a dog for walks," she said wistfully when she talked to her brother.

Thelma then reframed her reason for taking the job: "This is the move that will help me begin a career transition." She knew her company would not let her stay more than three years. She revised her goals, realizing she'd need to find a job in a company with headquarters in this city. She began organizing her work so she could spend fewer hours on the job. She joined the alumni club of her business school and a trade association. After meeting many people who had been forced to move to keep their jobs, Thelma decided she would consider starting her own business. Ironically, she realized, she would have to work on her career in order to develop the personal life she wanted. To her surprise, once she committed to her own business, she began to meet all sorts of interesting people, some of whom would become friends over the next year. "I think it was because I became focused that I met people focused on the same goals," she says. "We had something in common. Joining a hiking club was good for exercise, and the alumni group had some good speakers, but I realized that I began to make friends only after I stopped trying."

Richard found that he, too, began to develop a social life after he acknowledged that his move would be temporary. "I relaxed and stopped trying to enjoy the place," he said, "and I found all kinds of fun things to do here."

Knowing why you have moved can give you a strong sense of purpose, and you will come across as confident and attractive. "It's like a job," said Thelma. "When you walk around with an attitude like, 'Hey, I don't need this job,' you do good work and people will respect you. If the boss thinks you're one paycheck away from welfare, you'll get treated badly. Same with a social life. Walk around like, 'I like myself and I like being with myself,' and people can't stay away."

Reframe Aloneness as Solitude

To develop the confidence that comes from enjoying your own company, you have to view being alone as a positive, not a negative. "I was brought up to believe that I should always be doing things with other people," recalls Alice, the graphic designer. "Now I have learned that being alone gives me a lot of freedom. In fact, I need lots of time alone to work on my creativity."

British psychiatrist Anthony Storr (1988) reminds readers that love and friendship are important, but they are not the only sources of happiness. People also derive happiness from activities that they care about, anything from stamp collecting to gardening to painting. Solitude, Storr argues, gives people space to uncover their true selves, a process that is vital to creativity. When you lose yourself in a creative activity, you will feel energized and fulfilled. You will feel gloriously alone, not painfully lonely. The true pain of solitude comes not from the absence of interaction with others, but from sensory deprivation. People in solitary confinement or isolated for medical conditions often behave dysfunctionally because they lack access to views of the outdoors, to music, and other reassuring stimuli.

In her book, *The Artist's Way*, Julia Cameron recognizes that people who seek solitude for artistic pursuits need to replenish their creative resources. She urges people to take at least one solitary afternoon each week to gain new, stimulating experiences. You can use this time to visit a museum, walk through unfamiliar neighborhoods, give your undivided attention to a record album, see a movie, even wander through a shopping mall—anything that takes you away from your routine.

== Exercise
Celebrate Solitude

For the newcomer, spending some valuable time alone can be a powerful way for you to get in touch with your self-concept, to remind yourself of who you are, and to allow a gentle transformation of your identity as you grow into your new environment.

Take an afternoon off this week. I recommend afternoon because it is too easy to be distracted in the morning by what you have to do at work. What can you do this week that is just for yourself? Think of this time as a gift to yourself, a time of self-renewal. Think of three things that would leave you feeling refreshed and fulfilled.

After I work out at the gym, I head for the whirlpool. I feel that I am stealing the time. It is my gift to me.

I turn off the phone and play Beethoven. I put on the earphones and turn the sound up. I imagine I am conducting the orchestra. I have to be alone to do this!

Try to do this once a week. Make a point of doing something different each week. You'll find that this is a great way to replenish the energy reserves.

Plan for Periods of Loneliness

Every newcomer will experience hours, even days, of loneliness. You've called all your friends but nobody answers. You've been to the gym, walked the dog, gone to the movies (alone!), and signed up for a class. Now it's eight o'clock and you really want to be around people, but where do you go? A bar? A coffee shop? A singles event at the local church?

Loneliness is not the same as solitude. Unlike those in solitude lonely people feel that they have little choice about being alone. They feel powerless, and often stigmatized: "There must be something wrong with me!" At times like these, you'll be very vulnerable. Friends will not understand what you are going through unless they've been there themselves. It's easy to choose self-destructive distractions, such as eating, drinking, and turning yourself loose in the mall with your new credit card. You may find yourself spending hours in front of the television set, watching programs that seemed designed for people from another planet.

"I can't believe it," says Alice. "I started watching those shows about dating. I was fascinated. I had no idea they did this stuff. I was a zombie." "I played computer games and surfed the Internet for six hours at a stretch," says Richard. "When my wrists started to hurt, I realized something had to give. All I need is to get carpal tunnel syndrome right now."

These activities are not solutions, they're distractions. Instead of reinforcing your self-concept, they allow you to escape your self-concept and avoid thinking about your social identity.

═ Exercise ═══════════════════════════
I'm Lonely

Take some time to think about what it feels like to be lonely. By completing this worksheet you may discover some attitudes you didn't know you had.

When someone tells me she feels lonely, I think she must be

_____

When I wonder if he is lonely, I also wonder if he is _____

When I say, "I am lonely," what goes through my mind is

_____

I feel especially lonely when I _____

_____

because _____

What can I do to feel less lonely at these times? _____

_____

After you've noted your beliefs about loneliness, ask, Are these beliefs realistic?

Here's what Alice wrote:

I feel especially lonely when I'm eating dinner after work, because I feel like I am the only person in this city who is eating dinner alone. It's not normal to eat alone!

When Alice stopped to think about her beliefs, she realized, "I live in New York City. A lot of people are out there eating by themselves. Many people actually like eating alone!"

Keep a List of Self-Nurturing Activities

The concept of "comfort food," was discussed in chapter 4; foods like mashed potatoes and rice pudding remind many people of safe, comfortable childhoods. When you're feeling lonely, think of "comfort activities," things you can do to remind yourself of a time when you were safe and happy. Comfort food will fill your stomach for a few hours; comfort activities will fill your soul for days—and you won't consume a single calorie.

"I work out in the gym," says Marcie. "It's familiar. I don't care who else is there. I just feel great afterward. I bring my earphones and listen to my favorite comfort music. It's me." "I drive to the woods," says Lawrence, "and bring my binoculars. I hike and look at the wildlife and forget everything else for a while." "Bookstores!" said Jeff. "I go to those big megastores that serve coffee and the next thing I know, the afternoon is gone! I come home with ideas and a new outlook on life."

Should You Call a Friend When You Feel Lonely?

Close friends will want to support you through difficult times, but don't over do it. "An occasional call is crucial when you're new, when you need moral support," says Karen. "When the moving company destroyed my favorite chair, I called my best friend and cried. But I found that I sounded needy if I called too often. I learned to do things for myself, by myself, and call when I felt happy. Sharing good news will keep the friendship going."

Should You Adopt a Dog or Cat to Keep You Company?

If you love animals, says Jeff, there's no better solution. "A pet is a great ice-breaker. My dogs introduced me to all kinds of people, including someone special! And it's hard to feel lonely when a large furry object lands in your lap or wakes you up by licking your face."

Of course, adopting a dog or cat is not like signing up for woodworking class. A pet is for life! If you move, will you take your new friend along? If not, resist the temptation, a pet may not be the answer for you today. However, you may be able to offer your services as a foster pet parent. Some shelters need people to offer temporary care for animals who are recovering from surgery, are too young to place permanently, or have other special needs.

Should You Consider a Dating Service or a Single's Group?

Lana and Keith had independently come to the conclusion that they were ready to marry. They met through a dating service in Los Angeles, fell in love, sold their houses, and bought a larger house together—all in the space of a year.

Mina, newly divorced, had just moved to Atlanta, Georgia, when someone told her about a singles group at a local church. Mina called for information. "I was very direct," she says. "I told them I am not Christian. I am Moslem and I do not want to convert. Mina soon realized that she might not meet a new life partner, but she enjoyed making new friends, "especially women friends," she says. Unexpectedly, after a few pleasant months of activities, one of Mina's new friends said, "There is somebody you should meet. I think you'll like him." Six months later, Mina was married.

These stories have happy endings because Mina, Lana, and Keith were ready to marry. They knew what they wanted and they had realistic expectations. There is an old saying, "When the student is ready, the teacher will arrive." When people are ready to have an experience, they take steps, consciously or unconsciously, to make that experience happen. Mina's story emphasizes the importance of not feeling pressured. Mina says she would have been pleased with the group if she'd just continued making friends. The husband, she says, "was a bonus."

People who are comfortable with their own identity tend to enjoy single's groups. "When I was going through a bad patch after my divorce," says Ralph, "I couldn't hack it. Everybody seemed so aggressive and so determined to have fun. I had to drop out altogether for a while and do things by myself. I guess the secret is, if you don't need the group, you'll do fine."

Should You Seek Professional Help?

As chapter 6 suggests, you should consider professional help if you're responding dysfunctionally. If your loneliness interferes with your work, it might be better to seek help than to begin confiding in your new co-workers.

An ethical therapist will refuse to become your friend-for-hire, but rather will help you take the initiative to develop a system of social support. A therapist may offer you support and guidance, but you still have to take risks, reach out, and make the effort. And sometimes you will be lonely.

Exercise

The Solitary Evening

What can you do when you have a whole evening to fill?

If I just stay home, I can _____

I can walk to _____

I can drive or take a bus to _____

Plan to make the most of your solo time. You may discover that once you give it a chance, you enjoy spending time alone.

Alice decided she could feel less lonely by planning dinner as a special event, setting a table with her "company" dishes and place-mats. She could play music and appreciate her own cooking and her new home. Len, who hated to cook, chose to create a different kind of evening. He would watch the news or read the newspaper during dinner, and then take his dogs for a walk afterward. "It's my transition time," he said.

Internet Moving Tip

Search Moving Companies

Search the websites of a few major moving companies. Begin by typing the moving company's name into your favorite search engine. Moving company websites will include packing tips and other useful information. When you move, you may also be able to track the status of your shipment on the Internet. That is, if you haven't packed your computer.

12

"Take This Job and Move It!"

The Corporate Move

Changes in Identity

So your company has decided you need exposure to Flint, Michigan. Perhaps you decided to accept that job in Oklahoma City, and the company will pay your way. Congratulations! You have a great benefit. Not only will you save some financial pain, but you will also be able to maintain all three building blocks of your identity far more easily than if you moved on your own. The parts of your identity that relate to your job will be largely unchanged. At the same time, you may find yourself facing new conflicts as you try to balance the three building blocks of identity as they pertain to the other parts of your life. When you move, your identity statement, "I am a successful corporate manager," may conflict with, "I am a caring family member."

Self-Concept

People spend many hours at work. It's a familiar story, like the police officers who say they spend more time with their partners than their wives. People sometimes speak of a career as a vocation. Some of your "I am" statements probably relate to your job. "Since I moved, I feel like a stranger at home," says Lorraine. "But when I go to work and see the familiar logo of my company and talk on the phone to the same people at headquarters, I realize I'm the same person that I was before I left."

Harold, a university professor, keeps the same professional network when he changes jobs. "I'm in a small field," he says. "We all see each other at the same conferences, and we've been seeing each other since grad school. We read each other's papers and we talk on the phone or send e-mails. Even if I move to another university, it's like old home week when I go to a conference."

Social Identity

"Who are you?" often gets asked as, "What do you do?" and that means, "What is your job?" Therefore you may not experience a complete disruption of your social identity when you move with a corporation. "Whether I lived in Chicago or Houston or Birmingham, I could say, 'I'm a CPA,'" says Alice. "And I felt that people responded to me, each time, as a professional person."

People also respond to your corporate affiliation. Even if your neighbors don't work for Mega-Big Corporation, they probably know the local company's reputation. As a newcomer, you may gain an instant image as a solid, reputable person. "I moved into a conservative, neighborhood because I wanted a nice, safe place to live," says Alonzo. "At first my neighbors were put off because the way I dress is anything but conservative and I showed up at a party with my silver earrings. The new neighbors thought I was weird until they learned that I work for a big company and I'm in the Air Force Reserves."

On the other hand, some people find that the conversation dies when they announce their career affiliation. Roberta told me, "People sometimes get intimidated if I tell them I teach at the local university. So I start out by saying I'm a teacher." Edwin joined a corporation right after a bitter strike had ended. "The whole town was divided about supporting the strike," he says. "All I had to do was say I work for X Corporation and the conversation headed south."

Paper Identity

Your company connection can transform your paper identity. Company clout for a moving company transforms you from an individual person to someone the moving company needs—a valued, repeat customer. Your employer's reputation may also help you obtain housing and credit. "When we moved to this city," says Lillian, "I went to the bank. As soon as I told them my husband worked for the company he did, they couldn't do enough for me. My husband's company is big here; the name opens a lot of doors."

Renting an apartment or buying a house will be much easier when you move with a company. It's easier to document a salary history than it is to prove freelance income. Your credit history is strengthened if you can show continuous employment, especially with the same firm. "I value my individual identity," says Jim, "but I notice I get more respect when I pull out the company credit card. It's all about power. My company has a lot more clout than I do. I may not be around forever, but the company will."

Conflicts in a Corporate Move

Corporate moves come with their own set of identity interruptions. Inevitably, corporate values and demands will conflict with your own values and demands associated with family and other parts of your personal identity.

Family Identity vs. Corporate Identity

Nearly everyone who has studied, experienced, or advised others about corporate moves will agree: The greatest challenges arise from the conflicting needs of family members. "The company views me as Christopher's wife," says Laurel, "and, as Christopher's wife, I'm sort of a shadow figure, hovering in the background. Part of my identity comes from being Christopher's wife, but I'm also Laurel. I'm a mother, a community activist, a painter, and a freelance graphic artist. I'm also vice president of our neighborhood association and sometime coach of the junior high girls' softball team. Every single one of those parts of me will be lost if we make this move." As discussed in chapter 10, your children's identity can also be tied to your residence and therefore will be disrupted by a move.

Corporate attitudes are changing. Today, fewer companies view a corporate wife as an appendage to be moved at the whim of her husband. Indeed, the wife herself may be the person who is being relocated. Some firms help the relocated spouse find a job in the new community, while many have relocation packages.

Regardless of how much effort a corporation puts forth, however, each person and each family faces identity conflicts. If these conflicts are not resolved before the move, you may find yourself dealing with anger and frustration that escalate beyond repair. People sometimes lose their marriages or their jobs or both. Some find the gulf created by moving is simply too wide to overcome. You may need to seek guidance from professional counselors or from others who have moved. Some firms will pay for the assistance of relocation specialists as well as mental health support resources.

"Your age and the family's life cycle can also play a part," says Laurel. "When Christopher was just starting out, I was home with the babies. It didn't matter if we moved; in fact, I was happy because we got a bigger house and more money for the baby-sitter. Chris could move happily for a small step up the ladder.

"Ironically," Laurel continues, "Christopher's next move will be the big one, if it happens. If he's asked to move at all, he'll be a Regional Vice President. He'll get all sorts of perks and bonuses. Even if he never makes another move, he'll have achieved something in his career. Yet this move will be the most costly for everyone else in the family. The kids are finishing high school or starting college, and I've got my own life. We really don't need a bigger house."

=== Exercise ===
Know the Rules

Review your company's written policies on moving. If you will be moving as a family, any family member may want to complete this exercise also. Find out what benefits are offered to family members and what benefits are offered to the employee.

Now, before going further, write down your own interpretation of these policies: What are they really saying?

Stop! Read what you have written. What do your answers reveal about your feelings? For example, you need to get clear on how you feel about these policies. If you resent the business, you may find yourself taking it out on your family when they protest a move you feel is unfair.

> *They don't give a damn about their people. Everything in this policy is about what will not be covered. It's like they're begrudging us everything.*

> *We advertise ourselves as a family-friendly company that makes a range of products for every family member. Yet when it comes to our employees, we don't give a damn. Moving with your spouse? Pay your own way! Need an extra week to get settled? Forget it. We need you, body and soul, from Day 1.*

> *Ian's offer letter just dazzled us. They've paid for a consultant to help me find a job and they're offering extra compensation to make up for the income I'll lose after we move. I may go back to school and prepare for a new career!*

Benefits That Don't Help You

You need to make sure your company's policy can fit your unique needs. Ralph was lucky: "We have very generous benefits for relocation. The company paid for my wife and me to go visit Detroit before we signed the deal. They paid for two house-hunting trips. They moved me, my wife, the kids, and the dog, and I got lots of time off to help the kids get settled in school."

Charlene tells another story. "I used to work for Ralph's company," she says. "And sure, we had all those benefits. The problem is, those benefits didn't do a thing for me. I am a divorced single parent. What I needed was child care and extra money to pay a housekeeper and a handyman."

While some employers offer flexible benefits, many simply assume people arrive in opposite-sex pairs, sometimes with children attached. But the single person who moves an apartment with a small dog will not have the same needs as the family of five that moves an eight-room house, two cats, and a large dog. In their study of employees who relocated in Britain, Munton (1993, 31) found that the highest satisfaction and least stress were associated with flexibility. When individual relocation packages were designed to fit individual needs, employees were considerably more pleased than if they felt they were subject to standardized regulations. People were irritated by long lists of petty restrictions.

Few employers offer a lump sum of money for employees to use as they please—pay a professional moving company, take an extra house-hunting trip, spend a month in a local hotel while house-hunting, or even bring along an extra support person. While all sorts of benefits can be negotiated on an individual basis, a flexible policy would ease the transition for everyone. "I live in a small apartment," says John, newly divorced, "with very little furniture. The moving van cost a few thousand dollars. What I really needed was extra time for apartment-hunting, phone calls, and an extra trip home to take care of business."

Corporate policies often allow spouses to accompany managers on house-hunting trips and, of course, the move. As companies begin to offer benefits to same-sex partners, some gay couples are now able to both go along on house-hunting trips. Single, unattached people often need other family members, especially parents to help them move (Munton 1993). When family members are not available, a good friend can help enormously. For single people, the isolation during a move can seem intolerable, and having help can make all the difference.

"If I'd been married," says Gina, "my husband could have come along at the company's expense. As it was, I had to pay the airfare for my brother Ken to spend a few days with me. He helped put bookcases together, shopped for supplies, and mostly just lent moral support." A custom-designed relocation package, or a package offering considerable flexibility, shows respect and offers the individual a sense of control throughout a difficult process.

Making the Corporate Move

Now that you've seen how your corporate move can affect the rest of your life, you can look at how the move affects the job itself. When your identity is shaken up, things that once came easily can now seem like a chore. Moving brings many changes and difficulties that can affect how you do your job.

"Can We Go Yet?"

Once you know you have to move, your life gets put on hold. Chapter 1 emphasized that interruptions to identity can cause stress.

While you are waiting, you experience an extended interruption. Vince said, "I knew I'd have to move after two or three years, but I didn't know where. First they told me Chicago. We got psyched for Chicago. Then they said maybe Los Angeles. The date kept getting pushed back and our lives were put on hold."

"I Don't Have Enough Time!"

Moving gobbles up time. You have to pack, organize, change addresses, sort through possessions, deal with movers, find new housing, and a whole lot more. Once in a new home, for the first six months, everything takes longer. Everything has to be unpacked and organized in your new home. Getting ready for work and getting the children ready for school takes longer. Nearly everybody has conversations that go like this: "Did we unpack the iron?" "I think so. Did we put it in the bedroom closet?" "No, it's in the pantry—I think."

"I'm Late to Everything."

A wrong turn in an unfamiliar city can cost an hour. Newcomers don't know how to avoid the tie-up at the railroad crossing or the drawbridge that stays up for twenty minutes at a time. They get into lanes that force them off the freeway, stranding them in sections of town they've never heard of. "It was so embarrassing," says Marilyn. "I don't have a terrific sense of direction to begin with, yet here I am, a new director, and I got lost going to the company orientation. Fifteen miles from my office turned into a two-hour tour of the city after I took a wrong exit."

What disturbed Marilyn most was the interruption to her self-concept. She had always prided herself on being calm, competent, and organized. She was concerned about her social identity. Was she presenting herself as a frazzled person who was always late to meetings? These impressions, she knew, could linger a long time.

Munton (1993, 17) emphasizes the need for a "reasonable" workload. Yet people differ on what is "reasonable." Everyone who was interviewed for this book said, "I could have used time off during the move."

While experiencing this time pressure, your social identity will be fragile and you will be concerned with protecting your job, which constitutes a large part of your paper identity. Therefore, most newcomers resist complaining or asking for help. "I was just tired," says Jerome, a single parent. "In between business calls, I'd be getting calls from my son's school, the real estate agent, and the moving company.

It was hard to concentrate on anything, but I was reluctant to say anything. I was new and had to prove myself."

"I'm Not Myself at Work."

People who have been selected for transfer have usually demonstrated qualities associated with achievement. Yet soon after relocation, they may find themselves asking, "Did somebody make a mistake?"

Those who relocate will work at 70 to 80 percent of normal efficiency for the first six months (Munton 1993). This sub-par work performance can add further stress to the mover. At work the stress can manifest itself as irritability, absent-mindedness, and withdrawal—all behaviors that can be interpreted as incompetence or "poor attitude." Achievers who have become accustomed to viewing themselves as winners must now deal with lack of confidence. "I can't believe I asked so many dumb questions," recalls Sally. "I was just so disconcerted by the whole experience. The moving company was late and I had to go out and buy clothes to wear to a big meeting. I felt as though I were wandering around in a daze, and indeed I was."

The Corporate Social Life

A manager's wife once wrote to an advice columnist, complaining that she'd spent hours preparing for an employee party she and her husband were hosting, and not one employee wrote to thank her. The columnist agreed: the employees were rude. I sometimes wish I'd written my own letter, because I disagree. Social events are business events. When a manager invites the staff, they often feel obligated to attend, just as they would feel obligated to attend a staff meeting. Do they thank the manager for a meeting? Usually not, and usually they recognize a party as an extension of the workday. Indeed, managers sometimes charge the company for refreshments and cleaning expenses.

A welcome event has a purpose: to facilitate interaction among new employees. It is a business activity. Some people welcome these activities. "It was great," says Sally. "I met the wives of my colleagues and when they saw me and met my husband, they relaxed. They realized I'm not a threat."

But these events may come at a time when the new employees already feel overloaded. Often these events take place on weekends, are held at inconvenient locations, and require some form of business or "business casual" attire. While recognizing that the organizers may be attempting to be kind and hospitable, many employees view corporate social events as intrusions into their lives. Genevieve recalls, "I'm a new meeting coordinator and I sometimes have to travel with the executives to conferences. Most of the women executives were great. But when I went to the mandatory welcome dinner, the wives of the men stared daggers at me. It was like, 'We're home changing diapers and you're gallivanting off to New York.'"

Justin felt left out. "I didn't feel comfortable bringing my partner to the first welcome party. I have very little in common with my colleagues. They're great to work with but I would prefer to stay home and put on some jeans and an old sweatshirt and go get a hot dog with Edward." "All I could think of," says Mary, a single parent, "was here I am, trying to find a place that will take a kid and a dog, and with my salary and expenses it's tough. We came at a bad time of year and the rental market is tight. So here I am visiting my boss's gorgeous home in an exclusive suburb. He bought this place ten years ago and even he couldn't afford it today. And then I go back to my temporary apartment and read the want ads. I'd rather have them use the money they spent on the party for some good relocation support."

"I just wish they'd waited," says Genevieve. "After a few months, I knew everybody and I was settled into the community. I could even bring a date. This first party did more harm than good." "Let's face it," Justin says wryly, "if you're not half of a traditional married couple, a company party can seem more like a penance than a privilege."

═══ Exercise ═══
Social Studies

It can be helpful to anticipate the social responsibilities you'll have at your new job. By planning for problems you may be able to avoid them.

What social requirements will be associated with your move or transfer?

What images come to mind when you visualize yourself attending these events? Do you see yourself standing off to one side, holding an unwanted drink? Are you fending off personal questions while trying to ignore the knot in your stomach? Or do you see yourself as an enthusiastic participant who enjoys meeting new people?

If your images are negative, can you change your experience? Or can you avoid the event altogether?

Here's what some other corporate movers wrote:

> As a new person, I decided I was playing a part. I was like an actress who had to walk on stage and communicate her character by costume and nonverbal gestures. Who would I be? I wrote a little script and carried it with me. For the first time, I enjoyed a party at a manager's house.

> Every time I get transferred there's a reception at the regional manager's house for all the new employees. One year I realized that going to these events won't add a dime to my paycheck or affect a tenth of a point of my performance review. So I RSVP'd regrets and have been doing that ever since."

A final word on corporate social life: It gets better! "I hated all that stuff when I moved here," said Bridget. "It was my first job out of business school and I was nervous about what to say. I felt like a foreigner. Now I've been here five years and I organize the parties. I try to remember what was hard for me, so I keep things informal and I make sure people know that they don't have to go. But people usually show up, probably because we encourage them to wear blue jeans and sneakers and to bring their family. We serve fun food. One year it was pizza and one year we got out a hot dog stand. It's low-key and I think people appreciate that. We make it clear we'd rather spend money on relocation than party food. But still, even with all the effort to make the new people comfortable, it's usually more fun for the organizers than for the newcomers. We're relaxed and they're tense."

Do You Really Have to Move?

Occasionally creative negotiations pay off and you get to stay home. If you will be doing a great deal of travel, the company may not care where you live, as long as you come to the office for meetings. If your move will be temporary, you may be able to convince the firm that the cost of flying you in for an occasional meeting will probably be less than the cost of a full household move. A combination of tele-commuting and a negotiated schedule—"three days a week in the of-fice"—may allow you to remain where you are. Your employer also saves the overhead cost associated with your office: space, furniture, and lighting. When you're home, you buy your own coffee and heat it up with your own electricity, and your car doesn't occupy a space in the parking lot. If your company will fly you in for a sales call or to attend a meeting, you don't need a home base.

If you're an employer, you may want to ask your employees just how much more is accomplished by being in the office than by remaining at home. With the capabilities of telephone conference calls, voice mail, e-mail, and fax, you may find people are more pro-ductive at home, no matter whether that home is in Alaska, Arizona, or Atlantic City.

Internet Moving Tip

What's Available

There are two ways to check rental listings and houses for sale:

Type "apartment rentals" or "home sales" into your favorite search engine. You may find properties listed for your destination city, or you may not. Those listed tend to be truly unique.

Obtain the name of the local newspaper of your destina-tion city. Nearly all newspapers make the classified sections available online. You may even be able to place your own "rental wanted" ad via e-mail.

13

"I'm a Foreigner?!"

The International Move

You're moving abroad. Perhaps your company has arranged a foreign assignment. Perhaps you managed to qualify for employment in a company that is owned and operated by citizens of another country. How do you anticipate your move? It could be the dream of a lifetime or your worst nightmare. Maybe you're just gritting your teeth because you have no choice and you have to go.

Expressing Your Identity in a Foreign Accent

You have already seen how identity interruptions create stress. Researchers who study relocation consistently find that stress increases as geographic distance grows. They've found that adolescents who move to another city report greater stress than those who move to another section of the same city (Raviv et al. 1990); and families who move greater distances report greater stress (Munton 1990). Stress also increases when distance is measured by social and cultural patterns rather than miles (Hempel and Ayal 1977). When you move to a new country, you will almost certainly experience cultural and social distance even if you move just a few miles across a border.

"It's Almost the Same"

Electronic communications have changed the face of the earth. If you walk down the main street of nearly any major city, you will see familiar signs that advertise familiar brands of soft drinks, fast food, and clothing. Traffic signs have become internationalized. You can follow American news stations as you travel around the world. Most likely, you won't have to miss an episode of your favorite sitcom, and you'll wait only a short time for the release of Hollywood movies to theaters near you. Yet beneath the commercial similarities, you will find differences in even the most mundane aspects of daily life.

- Catch a cold? Last time I visited a Scandinavia country, I couldn't buy popular symptom-relieving cold remedies. I had to survive on aspirin and vitamin C. Other countries allow you to buy potent medication that is available only by prescription in the United States.

- Waiting for a bus? Did you know that you have to stand in line in London and in some former British colonies? You'll need to find out how to buy a ticket and get it validated, and you risk a fine if you don't get it right.

- How cold is it? Twenty degrees Celsius? Sounds a bit chilly. If you are from the United States, you may need a few moments to realize that twenty degrees Celsius is positively balmy.

These simple differences will remind you every day that you are living in a foreign country. While being a tourist can be confusing, becoming a resident lets you experience daily life in the local culture. You may be fascinated or repelled by what you find, but you will definitely be transformed.

"I Didn't Know I Was ..."

Chapter 3 suggested some exercises to help you decide whether you could maintain your identity in a new environment. When you move internationally, you become aware of aspects of your identity that you have always taken for granted.

═ Exercise ═════════════════
Who Am I in Another Country?

Before you move, it can be helpful to think about how living in another country might change you.

Return once again to your "I am" statements from Chapter 1. Will any of these statements change after you move?

Now imagine that you have been living in the new country for six months to a year. Who will you be? Complete these ten statements:

1. I am _____

2. I am _____

3. I am _____

4. I am _____

5. I am _____

6. I am _____

7. I am _____

8. I am _____

9. I am _____

10. I am _____

How do you feel as you read them over?

Anticipating a move to Europe, Wilma's answers included "gaining valuable career experience" and "developing a new appreciation of art and music," but she also wrote that she'd feel "isolated and lonely" and "very busy." Joel, who planned a trip to teach English in Japan, wrote "saving money," "having a great social life," and "learning the language."

─────────────────────────────────

You may not be able to answer these questions before you leave. Many people are surprised not only by what they find, but also by their own reactions to new and unfamiliar surroundings. How many aspects of your identity will change when you move? If you move with your family while keeping your current employer, you'll probably find that many of your roles will continue, but you can also expect some surprises.

Keep your list and review it after you've lived abroad for a while. You may realize you're meeting a lot of your early expectations, or you may realize your experience differs a great deal from what you thought it would be.

Social Identity

Regardless of your citizenship, you probably take your national identity for granted. Your "I am" statements probably did not include, "I am a member of the dominant culture," yet moving from majority to minority can change every aspect of your identity. Newcomers who find themselves suddenly thrust into minority status have reported increased stress (Padillo 1986). Now you can be called an immigrant, a non-citizen, a temporary resident. How do you feel when these words are applied to you?

You may also have to explain or defend the stereotype of your home country. For example, saying "I am an American" can bring out strong reactions all over the world. Others may express hostility or resentment. People may say wistfully, "I wish I could move there." Paul, who was born and raised in Toronto, recalls, "In the 1980s, I went to graduate school in New England. I was surprised to learn how many Americans thought Canada was wonderful. They expected me to be smart and polite because I'm Canadian."

On the other hand, says Mona, "when I moved to Spain, people were horrified to learn that I was from New York. They had trouble believing that I had never even witnessed a street crime. They even asked me if I carried a gun."

Cultural Values

Local customs may challenge your own personal values. Helen was flying on the local airline of a small Eastern European country. She was shocked when the uniformed agent demanded $200 extra for the luggage and supplies she carried. Helen's co-worker Mark, who had been working in that country for five years, quietly asked, "Is there anything we can do about that?" Before Helen knew what was happening, Mark handed the agent a twenty-dollar bill. They took off with the luggage and the episode was never mentioned again.

Some people would feel violated by this transaction. Others accept and even enjoy it as part of the flavor of another country. Your employer may have guidelines that may bring you in harmony—or in conflict—with these local customs.

Learning your way around a new culture can be difficult because people tend to take their own value systems for granted. Often the natives are surprised when foreign visitors ask for explanations of local customs.

Jane, an American living in Canada, was horrified to learn about her Canadian friend's encounters with a government agency. "Why don't you write your senator?" Jane asked. "That's what I'd do back home."

"We don't think like that," said her Canadian friend. If you had asked the Canadian woman to describe the culture, she would not have said, "We respect bureaucracy and don't press for change." Yet when questioned, she was able to clarify her values immediately.

Your Paper Identity

When you move to another country, you become aware of the way your identity is expressed through documents.

Your Career

A major part of your paper identity comes from your job and your status as an employee. Yet in a new country, you or your spouse may not be allowed to work. When Trish accompanied her husband Alex overseas, she took a leave of absence from her job as an elementary school teacher. In her new country, she was surprised to learn that she could not even serve as a volunteer in the local school system until her work visa had been approved. "Being dependent on Alex's income was new to me," said Trish, "and anyway there wasn't much to do all day. We weren't in a large capital city and everybody in the neighborhood was either working or home with their kids all day."

As you reveal information to the immigration authorities, you may become frustrated with the bureaucracy and also feel vulnerable due to the lack of privacy. Every aspect of your life will become subject to scrutiny as the host government decides if you deserve to be given residency privileges.

"Will You Be a Drain on Our System?"

If you work in a country for more than a few months, you probably need to obtain a resident visa. Visa applications typically require you to disclose nearly all of your personal, medical, and financial information. You must disclose the possessions and money you are bringing into the country. You may even have to take a medical examination from an authorized doctor. The report will then be scrutinized and interpreted by faceless bureaucratic agencies. The immigration authorities often write to police agencies and the FBI to see if you have a criminal record. Your employer may be given information about the results of any investigation, and you may have little control over the confidentiality of your records.

Even if your private information is not shared with your employer, any unusual finding may delay your application and cause raised eyebrows among your colleagues. A child's early illness, your own childhood hospitalization, or a recent operation may require additional reports or examinations that may not be covered by your insurance. Some medical conditions will prohibit your entry altogether.

Obtaining Information

On an international move, you often experience an additional layer of stress when you try to obtain information about the legal aspects of your move. Most people are not familiar with the immigration and residency laws of their own country. Even the most well-meaning people will not be able to advise you unless they have personal experience with your situation. For instance, an ethical, careful financial advisor may not think of advising you about tax consequences of transferring investments to the United States after you return home. He or she may never have faced that situation before.

You need to get information from as many people as possible. You will be surprised at the variation among the answers you get. The cost of living may be described as "outrageous" or "not bad if you know the system" or even "extremely reasonable." If you are moving on your own, you may be advised to seek help from an immigration lawyer; or you may be told that a lawyer is a waste of money.

If you can find government officials to answer your questions, you may still obtain conflicting information. Ted wanted to ship his two cats into the United States. He was told that (a) he must have a health certificate for each cat; (b) current regulations require only the customs officer's judgment about the animal's appearance ("looks fine to me!"); and (c) although (b) is accurate, the rules haven't been distributed yet, so follow (a) just in case.

Maintaining Your Self-Concept

Moving to a new country represents a major identity interruption. When you first arrive, you may find it easier to deal with the interruption by maintaining ties to your home country. Following are some ways to feel connected.

Use the Internet

You can stay connected electronically from nearly every corner of the world. Your hometown website will be accessible from Indiana to Istanbul. With a few keystrokes, you can keep up with local elections, football teams, and comic strips. You can browse your hometown newspaper for the cost of a connection.

Bring Your Favorite Books and Music

Even if you continue to speak your native language, you will hear different accents and even different music. Listening to your favorite music while reading your favorite novel can take you back home on a lonely evening.

Too much local music? Remember that cultures differ with regard to tolerable noise levels. A set of earplugs can help you stay sane in a small apartment with thin walls

Plan Your Connections

E-mail and fax are usually the cheapest and fastest way to stay in touch with friends and family. Mail can be slow and even a small parcel can be delayed in customs. If you need to send something fast, choose one of the private carriers, such as FedEx, UPS, Airborne Express, or DHL. A parcel sent via United States mail will be turned over to the post office of the destination country, and may therefore be subject to delays.

Arrange for Visits

When you need to hear a familiar voice, remember that telephone rates have been dropping. Often calls placed from the United States will be considerably cheaper than those initiated abroad, so you may want to arrange to reimburse friends and family who call you. When nothing will take the place of a real live person, compare the cost of obtaining an airline ticket in both countries. The results may surprise you.

Medical Care

Americans will find new forms of medical care if they live abroad. If you work for a major company, you will probably have access to private care. You may even continue your United States health plan. If you work for a foreign employer, you may be required to participate in a national or regional health plan. When I talk to people who have lived abroad, many of them say that they were especially surprised at the difference in attitudes toward medical care.

Different Treatment Options

Bryan, a chemist working in Switzerland, burned his hand in the lab. The hospital encouraged him to bathe the arm in one kind of herb tea, and to drink vast quantities of other herbal teas. He interacted a great deal with nurses and even custodial staff: "They kept everything very, very clean," he said. The wound healed without a scar, but American visitors were horrified: "Back home you'd have had surgery and skin grafts and antibiotics!"

Mental Health Options

Mental health care may differ even more from one culture to another. Some Canadian provincial health plans will reimburse only psychiatric services recommended by a physician. Private employers may offer supplemental coverage that allows people to see licensed psychologists or social workers.

Counseling services remain stigmatized in some countries. While Americans take for granted the need for counseling following divorce or bereavement, other cultures do not recognize this type of therapy as appropriate, let alone as a right.

Laws

Before you move overseas, research the laws of your destination country. Some Middle Eastern countries place restrictions on the way women dress or whether they may drive cars. You may be asked not to photograph soldiers who are standing guard in an airport. You may be screened for jobs based on your age or marital status. In London, the cars, not pedestrians, have right of way, except in marked crosswalks.

Don't Even Think of Breaking the Laws of a Foreign Country

An executive from a large American communications company told a group of listeners, "One of our managers decided to steal a watch from a store in Saudi Arabia. We have no idea why. He earned a good salary and could easily buy his own watch. In Saudi Arabia, the stores remain unlocked because the penalties for stealing are so severe."

Indeed they were: the man's hand was cut off. The company's powerful staff of lawyers tried to intervene, but the best they could get was a compromise: the hand could be removed surgically by a doctor in a private setting. The company gave the man an artificial hand and a return ticket back to the United States.

Another manager, the executive continued, allowed his people to work on a religious holiday. The penalty was a ritual beating. Again, the company was unable to intervene. The Moral: If you don't think you can accept the laws of the country, don't go.

Social Norms

Sometimes it can be as difficult to learn the customs of a country as it is to learn the legal system. Canada is close by and most Canadians speak English, but after spending five years in Manitoba, I learned their customs can differ quite a bit. For example, Canadians tend to be very respectful of rules. At an international professional meeting, a Canadian speaker told a joke: "How do you get one-hundred Canadians out of a swimming pool?" After a pause, he shared the punch line: "Just say, 'Everybody out of the pool!'" Canadians laughed immediately, but most Americans didn't get it.

On a deeper level, countries differ with respect to human rights legislation, which in turn influences social norms. Some countries recognize only their own official religious holidays. You may therefore be expected to work on a day that you consider sacred.

Social customs often dictate a woman's behavior. Some cultures mandate conservative dress and manners for women. However, some countries actually offer women more social freedom than they would experience in some parts of the United States. Women in Scandinavia, a Danish colleague told me, have always smoked cigars and pipes. "And of course I go to bars alone," she added. "What's the big deal?"

What's Fair?

Americans tend to believe that people should be rewarded for their accomplishments, more or less in proportion to their success. This concept comes from the notion that fairness means equity. Some cultures subscribe to principles of equality rather than equity. In these cultures, employers tend to base rewards on impersonal factors, such as age or seniority, rather than attempt to evaluate contributions of employees. If you are living in a country with this culture, the government and private sector will be more concerned with providing a safety net at the bottom than a major reward at the top. You may find strong support for trade unions.

Both resources and rewards may be allocated in a manner that you may consider arbitrary. A Dutch professor, working at an East Asian university, told me that his department allocated travel funds to an "inner circle." "I've visited in American universities that did the same thing," he said, "but here it's considered the norm." Those who became frustrated with the system tended to leave after a year or two. Those who could laugh about it, or who enjoyed their own source of revenue, didn't object.

Reframing the International Experience

A great deal of your international experience will depend on the temporary identity you create for yourself as "expatriate" or "visitor." What will you tell the folks back home? What will you write in your journal and paste in your scrapbook? The most horrendous, hair-raising stories will become the tales you share most often. Some of my own adventures include being stranded at the airport in Kiev when I showed up to teach in an exchange program, and dealing with Customs while shipping cats and household goods to and from Canada.

It is easy to get caught up in everyday hassles with the Customs and Immigration services, the rules that you don't understand, the bureaucracy, and the taxes. These experiences are stressful and you may find yourself questioning your own identity. One effective way to develop a resilient, stress-resistant identity is to frame your experience to reflect your growth and possibly transformation. Following are some suggestions to keep yourself on track as you settle overseas.

Enjoy the Adventure

Try to find a flexible, resilient part of yourself that thrives on adventure. Olivia says her career goal always included travel. "When I get tired, I remember that I'm fulfilling a lifetime promise to myself."

Dick summed it up this way: "When I feel frustrated in my new community, I remember all the people who say, 'I wish I could do that.' Sure, it's frustrating to be a foreigner and travel back and forth, but a lot of people would kill to be able to do just that."

Savor the Experience

Every week, do something that you could not do if you were "back home." Visit a museum, a shopping area, or a sporting event. Take a day trip to go sightseeing. Even on a limited budget, you can explore the city. Sometimes a ride on a local bus can be an adventure in itself. For example, you may have enjoyed taking dance classes or playing basketball in a local league. Here, you may not have access to participation, but you may have easy access to world-class performances.

Develop a New Part of Yourself

Try to be open to new experiences you might not have had at home. At the end of your visit you can say, "I have been enriched by what I have learned." For instance, you've probably been told to learn the language as soon as possible. You may be able to absorb quite a bit simply by opening yourself to your new environment. Turn on the local radio instead of the compact disc player when you do household chores. If you know the local language, you may find activities for personal growth that would not be available at home.

Keep a Journal

If you have time, keep a record of your experiences. Even mundane exchanges will shed new light on the local culture. Here are some sample entries:

"I got in the cab when it was forty-below. The driver was a refugee from an African country, where he'd been a guerrilla fighter. He told me about his country on our drive crosstown. You just don't meet African freedom fighters back in Iowa."

"The city still has blue laws. On Sunday, supermarkets can only have four people on duty. I watched one elderly lady ask everybody why they couldn't operate at full capacity. She honestly didn't realize that Sunday was supposed to be a religious holiday. So much for local cultural uniformity."

Returning Home

If you return home, you will need to renegotiate your identity again. You'll have to re-learn the local customs and catch up on the ways your home country has changed. You may be delighted to be back or you may find yourself missing what you had overseas.

People may respond to you in a new way. You may become identified with your temporary country or you may be regarded as an expert. You may be stereotyped or stigmatized. If you are an American who has worked for a foreign employer, you may have to reassure prospective employers that you have the right to work in the United States. Your children may find they've gained or lost a grade in school. Teenagers can feel displaced from social groups.

Renegotiating your identity can take months, even years. When friends and acquaintances talk about the country where you lived, you may find yourself annoyed because they seem to be stereotyping. You may become disillusioned with the country and find yourself debunking positive beliefs about it. Or you may just be happy to get home.

═══════════ Moving Tip ═══════════

Moving Overseas

- If you're moving abroad, learn how investments are regulated in the destination country. When you return home, will you have to pay heavy penalties to withdraw your funds? Or can you withdraw them at all? Some retirement funds will be severely restricted.

- If you live overseas for more than a year, you may need to obtain a local driver's license. Find out if your home country, state, or province will accept that license as valid when you return home, so you won't have to take another test. Do not let your license expire while you're overseas! If your overseas license will not be accepted on return, ask the motor vehicle bureau to explain your options.

- When planning to leave a foreign country where you have been residing, learn what the host government defines as "residency." There may be different definitions for tax and immigration purposes.

14

"It's Their Turn
Now ..."

Helping Friends and Family Move

What if you're the one getting the phone calls? Your friends are moving from Boise to Boston and you live in San Diego. If you own this
book you probably have some experience with moving and know
what they're going through. Or maybe your friends lent you this
book in order to let you know what they're going through. Perhaps
you're the one moving from Boston to Boise and do not know how to
ask for help.

During a move, people become anonymous. Like an airplane in
flight or a ship on the high seas, they are known by numbers. To a
moving company, they're just a truck—or part of a truck—to be dis-
patched. To the real estate agents and rental property managers,
they're a potential source of revenue.

Friends and family can play a valuable role in this transition:
they can anchor the identity of their loved ones who move. Airplanes
have separate radio systems for communicating with the control

tower and with the company headquarters. When you stay in touch with your friends as they move, you're the contact with company headquarters, the home base. The local airport may provide emergency assistance, but ultimately it's the home base that offers the continuing contact with a familiar world that, in turn, provides a lasting thread of identity.

Why They Need You

How important are family and friends? A ship on the high seas can expect help from the Coast Guard when there is trouble. Even civilian ships give distress calls top priority. Helping a foundering vessel is the code of the sea. But when your friends move, they may find that the only rescuers they can turn to do not follow the code of the sea, but "the code of the pocketbook," as one disgruntled newcomer put it. People who seek help often find themselves besieged by offers from commercial sources, such as real estate agents and moving companies. While many of these individuals are ethical, your best interest is not their only priority. They also have obligations to their shareholders and owners. They may not have time to listen carefully or they may simply lack an understanding of your friend's needs. They may be high-pressure salespeople, or they may simply be feeling pressured themselves.

You can offer a familiar voice as your friend tries to negotiate unfamiliar situations. "The property management agent urged me to sign up for this apartment," said Julia. "He said there were very few places that I'd want to live in and that I'd have trouble finding anything better. So I signed up and I really regretted it. I hated the apartment! I found out there were lots of great places to live. Most of them did not go through property management agents. I'd like to think that my agent just didn't know, not that he fudged the truth. Either way, I got screwed."

"I wish," continues Julia, "that I'd had a friend to call. I wish someone had said to me, 'Now look, Julia, you've always found great apartments. You've got a gift for finding apartments! You have money. You don't need to rush. Real estate agents can exaggerate. Stop! Sleep on it! If the unit is gone tomorrow, it means you weren't supposed to have it. You won't live in the park.'"

Notice what Julia wanted. She wanted someone who knew the Real Julia, the Julia who was a gifted apartment hunter and who wasn't lacking for money. She wanted someone to tell her what she probably knew: it's dangerous to make decisions under pressure.

Julia knew all about sales appeals based on scarcity ("Last one! Buy now!"), but she was exhausted. She had three days to look for a place to live before she had to fly off again. A friend could have helped by warning, "Hey, put the brakes on. You've got time."

How You Can Help

If you're the one who's moving, you may want to share this chapter with a friend. You may also want to seek help in these areas before trouble strikes, building a support system you can depend on during the transition. If you're on the receiving end when someone like Julia calls, be prepared! Here's what you can do.

Be Sensitive to the Timing of Their Decisions

Sometimes you may have trouble finding anything positive to say about the destination city. What you say depends on whether your friend has made a commitment or is still deciding what to do. "It's like talking to someone who wants to get married," says Sharon, who lives in a city where people always seem to be moving in or moving out. "Before they're engaged, you want to be frank. In fact, I think there's an obligation to protect people from their own short-term enthusiasm. Warn them about all the hazards. But once there's a ring on the finger, you support the decision the best you can."

If your friend hasn't made a commitment definitely share your doubts about location, lifestyle, and housing options. Express your concerns about your friend, not about the city: "You seem to enjoy the beach so much and I don't think there's one in Louisville"; "I think of you as an urban person"; or "I really can't see you in a small house or an apartment; you need space!" People who are comfortable with the decision will not feel threatened. Those who become angry or resentful may realize they need to revisit some issues about their new location.

Help Friends Anticipate a New Identity

You can help friends develop positive expectations, even enthusiasm, by finding positive things to say about the destination city: "I've always wanted to live there"; "You'll be near the beach! I'm jealous"; or "You can get a dog."

Merge Past and Present at Farewell Parties

As a good friend or family member, you may want to organize a farewell gathering. These rituals help because they remind the mover,

"You were successful here. You're the same person and you can be successful again."

At the same time, you want to help the mover assimilate his or her new identity. While you reminisce about good times here, include some activities that direct attention to the future home. Encourage the guest of honor to share stories of moving to the new city. You might ask each guest to share some good news about the destination. You could rent a movie that was filmed in the destination city and show scenes that feature positive aspects of living there.

Should you joke about the destination city? If people are comfortable with the decision, they won't care. "I was going back to New York—finally," says Robert. "New York is home. I couldn't wait to move back. At my farewell party in Dallas, everybody gave me joke gifts, like a 'Muggers Keep Out!' T-shirt and a box of giant apples. I loved it."

Stella was less comfortable with the move, and therefore the jokes. "We were moving to Texas because John got such a great job we couldn't refuse. I was a little edgy about the idea. One of our friends served chili and cornbread, teasing, 'This is what you'll be eating from now on!' Actually, that was one of our deepest fears: greasy Southern food. When we moved down we were relieved to find lots of great places to eat. Our neighbors are even vegetarians! So now we can laugh, but we didn't back then."

Give Gifts That Ease the Transition

Gifts can express the identity of the current residence. A plaque or photograph can be displayed on an office wall to start conversations in the new location. Posters, sweatshirts, and other souvenirs can keep fond memories alive for a long time.

Gifts can also ease the hassle of moving. For instance, nearly everybody has to clean up a residence before they move. A cleaning service may seem like a luxury, but a few friends can chip in to make this service affordable. Almost any service will arrange a gift certificate. People need everything from clothing to carwashes when they move. And don't forget the most precious hassle-saving gift of all: your own time and energy. Offer to run errands, help with packing, or deliver meals.

Gifts can speed up the transition by getting your friend involved in their new location right away. When Harold left Montana to attend graduate school in Wisconsin, his friends called the bookstore in Wisconsin to order a gift certificate that he could use right away to buy books and supplies.

Psychologist Joan Lerner, whom I interviewed for this book, encourages friends to subscribe to arts at the new location. It's easy to procrastinate about obtaining tickets in the middle of a move, but you can help. Wendy's friends ordered a subscription to the ballet in her new city, knowing she'd love going but might put off getting the tickets. Joe's friends knew what Joe liked to eat. They did some research and ordered a gift certificate for an excellent Italian restaurant in his now hometown.

Keep Up the Momentum After the Party

Sometimes people have to remain in town longer than they planned. They need your support more than ever. Even if your friends leave on schedule, call on packing and moving day. People will be busy, so be sensitive to their time pressures. A brief "I'm thinking of you!" will help. "It's the loneliest feeling when the moving van pulls up," sighs Deirdre. "They come in and take over and shove your stuff around. I felt so intimidated."

Offer to perform real chores. Even the smallest chore can seem insurmountable during a move. "I had never gotten around to mailing this package," says Hal, "so we ended up packing it and taking it with us. If someone had called and offered to take it to the post office, I'd have been so grateful."

After the moving company takes the furniture, your friend may have to spend a night in a hotel or camped out on the floor of a bare apartment. This might be a good time to check in and let the movers know there is someone out there who's thinking of them. "It feels creepy to be alone in an empty house," says Helen. "I just wish someone had called to go out to dinner. They probably figured I'd be too busy."

Validate an Identity-in-Transit

Remember Julia, who rushed into renting an apartment? Her experience is not at all uncommon. People on the move feel anonymous, and they feel they are dealing with faceless, interchangeable, commercially oriented resources. When people feel overwhelmed by a new environment, they often feel out of control. In such situations, they may find themselves behaving irrationally, even self-destructively (Zimbardo 1991).

You can call your friend and remind him, "You're still the same person! I know you!" Even a single phone call can lend crucial support to your friend's identity and defuse some of the anxiety caused by the new surroundings.

Reinforce New Roles and Identities

When people move, they often try out new identities. Sometimes the identities seem uncomfortable because they don't fit with the person's past life: "If my friends could see me now!" A social identity consists not only of interactions with new people, but also of imaginary conversations with friends from the previous neighborhood. So, by approving your friend's choices, you'll support your friend's changing social identity. "When I moved to a suburban community in Kansas," says Kevin, "I felt that I was betraying my former self. I actually watch cable TV now! Then my sister called and said it's a sign of growth to try new things and I need a taste of popular culture anyway."

Translate New Experiences into a Familiar Language

One of the ways people find meaning in an experience—any experience—is to tell the story. Psychologists talk about "creating a narrative" as a way to deal with trauma. As you listen to friends tell their stories, you can help them translate their experiences into an idiom that's familiar to them. By sharing a point of view, you help your friends process their new experiences. "Yes, I'm meeting some wonderful new people," says Yolanda, who was enjoying her move from Chicago to Atlanta, "but I call my friend Judy every week. We talk about the people I've met and we joke about what I'm finding in Atlanta. When I say, 'The Marta transit system is like the El, only scrubbed clean and computerized,' she knows just what I mean."

Give Friends a Safe Place to Express Themselves

When the newcomers are too new to talk freely to the residents of the city, you can lend a familiar ear. "This is a very small town," says Nicki. "I was in culture shock. I couldn't say anything, of course, because everybody here just loves it, and I'm sure that eventually I will, too. But for now, I've budgeted a decent amount for phone bills so I can stay in touch with my friends."

Support Deeper Cultural Identities

If your friends feels like the only one, you can reach out and let them know they're not alone. "There were few African Americans here," says George, who moved with his wife to a Midwestern town to attend graduate school. "We felt very isolated. My brother would call every week and say, 'Hang in there! Don't you dare give up!'

And we'd talk about stuff we did together back in high school. It made me feel a lot better."

Reframe Negative Outcomes

Even if your friend chose a good location, she may have made a mistake with her job or her residence. Sometimes people just can't fit in no matter how hard they try. Friends can help reframe a mistake as "something that could happen to anybody," and not "the final proof that you're irrational." "I hate this condo!" Allen said when he called his friend John. "I can't believe I bought a home here. There are all kinds of fights and meetings and since I'm new, I get caught up in the middle. Every time I leave work, I get stressed all over again."

John understood. "My parents had the same problem," he said. "My dad moved to a condo after he retired. They took a big loss to move for the same reason—the neighbors were always fighting. Condos work for some people but not everybody."

Visit Your Friends—but Not Too Often

Visits can offer crucial support during the first year. When I compare stories of happy and unhappy newcomers, I find that those who have relocated successfully have had several visits from family and friends. Of course, there are many factors that could explain this phenomenon. People with close connections may have better social skills. People who are happy with their new homes may be more likely to invite visitors. Indeed, one woman told me, "I'm embarrassed to invite anyone to this city!"

Regardless, new arrivals usually appreciate visits from friends and family. Even casual friends can become welcome reminders of a familiar identity. If at all possible, try to visit those who have moved, rather than encourage them to come to you. When you visit, you reinforce their new identities. Just make sure you respect their space. They may not be ready for visitors yet, so let them know you're open to the possibility. Chances are they'll be inviting you down before you know it.

Don't forget that a telephone visit won't cost your friends a dime and will be considerably less disruptive than a personal visit. Call right after they've moved to see how they're doing. Call friends and relatives on special occasions, especially birthdays and holidays. Call just to say hello.

When You Visit, Be Understanding

Don't expect your loved ones to entertain you. "Look, I adore my buddies," says Don. "But Sheryl and I had just moved to Denver.

We were broke. We'd spent more on the move than we expected and the car died just as we got to town. Sheryl was pregnant and we had to save money. Then my brother Ralph comes to town, and he wants to eat steak every night. He wants to go sightseeing and see the mountains. I had to work. Sheryl was setting up the house and trying to find a temporary job. If he'd stayed three days and eaten hamburgers, it would have been fine. But he wanted to stay a week and he'd have stayed more if I'd let him."

Irene, who is single, agrees. "I always made time for friends and wished I had more visitors," she says wistfully. "But after a while it got awfully expensive. Even though they stayed at a hotel and paid their way, it costs a lot to eat dinner in restaurants every night."

If You Visit, Share Your Feelings Judiciously

Once a friend—I'll call him Ted—visited me when I was holding down a temporary job in a small Northeastern city. I was delighted to see him, as I hadn't lived there long enough to make friends and knew I'd be leaving in a few months. Unfortunately, Ted was in a particularly critical mood. "These people are really ugly," he said. "And look how they dress." When we went out to dinner, he complained again. "They didn't chill the salad forks," and "The bread is ordinary." My subleased apartment was dismissed as "dark and gloomy." I was never enthused about living in that city, but Ted's visit did nothing to raise my spirits. I realized that Ted was going through a difficult time himself, and perhaps I'd been a little too enthusiastic when I encouraged him to visit. However, I found myself wishing he'd stayed home until he felt better.

Encourage Friends and Relatives to Visit You—but Not Too Persistently

"I have three sisters," says Manuel, "and my wife comes from a big family, too. Every year it's a hassle: Do we visit the relatives in California, or the ones in Ohio, or the ones in Washington, D.C.? We just don't have the money or the time to visit everybody. We have three children and, no matter how we do it, travel is tough."

Some families rotate Christmas visits, while others organize a big reunion in a central location. You can also plan individual celebrations, or exchange cards and phone calls. When friends or family members can't show up for a holiday or a wedding, be understanding. They probably regret their absence as much as you do. You may want to pour on the pressure, but usually the only outcome is the deterioration of your relationship.

Because each situation is unique, you'll probably have to design activities to fit each friend or family member as well as each destination. Here are some exercises to help get you started.

═══ Exercise ═══
Helping with The Decision

If the decision has not been made, you can help your friend make the right choice.

Imagine your friend or family member in the location under consideration. You may want to visualize your friend living there, or you may write a narrative.

What comes to mind? Do you see your friend fitting in or resisting? Happy or miserable, or somewhere in between?

_____

_____

_____

How can you tactfully express your concerns? Consider writing what you might say.

_____

_____

_____

What reaction do you anticipate?

_____

_____

_____

If the friend or family member has made a commitment, think of three positive statements that offer encouragement. For example,

It'll be cold, but the winter nights are beautiful.

The shopping is fantastic.

1. _____

2. _____

3. _____

Just remember that your goal is to be as supportive as you can. Think what you'd like to hear if the roles were reversed.

═ Exercise
Planning the Farewell Party

The party should be as much a celebration of the future as it is an acknowledgment of the past.

Think of three activities for a farewell party that would merge past and future. Ask yourself what your loved one would enjoy. Some people love party games, others abhor them. If you like games, perhaps everyone could think of something to look forward to that begins with a certain letter of the alphabet. If you're avoiding games, perhaps you could prepare a special cake to celebrate the transition—a map with lines drawn between two cities? A poster symbolizing the move? These suggestions are meant to stir your creativity. Ultimately, the program you plan yourself will be the most effective.

1. _____

2. _____

3. _____

═ Exercise
Thoughtful Gifts

Think of some gifts that will help friends in their new location. A guidebook to the city? A gift certificate at a store or restaurant? A gift certificate for a cleaning service or home organizer? What would you like if you were moving?

1. _____

2. _____

3. _____

Relationships are very important for people in transition. The support of a good friend or a close family member can mean the difference between disaster and success for these stressed out movers. During a time when their identity is challenged by new people and places, it is reassuring to know that someone understands their plight. By lending a hand, or even a sympathetic ear, you let your loved ones know that no matter where they move, they have friends and family out there who know and love them, that though surroundings may change, some things are permanent. If you remember your own stressful move, why not share what you learned with a loved one who is about to embark on a similar journey. A little help can make a big difference.

Internet Moving Tip

Virtual Library

Numerous books are available to help you deal with moving. If you search www.amazon.com with keywords "relocation" and "household moving," you'll get a huge selection of choices that may not be available locally. Many of these books are written for children. You may be especially fortunate to learn that a guide has been published for your destination. For example:

Arizona in Your Future: The Complete Relocation Guide for Job Seekers, Retirees and Snowbirds by Betty Martin and Don Martin (Pine Cone Press, 1998).

Relocating to San Francisco and the Bay Area: Everything You Need to Know before You Go and Once You Get There by Cristina Guinot (Prima Publishers, 1996).

Newcomer's Guide to Chicago by Mark Wukas and Thor Ringler (First Books 1998). Similar titles are available for Los Angeles and Minneapolis.

And my personal favorite:

What Sucks About South Florida: The Travel-to, Move-to Guide, by Scott Marcus, (Fender Publishing Company, 1997).

References and Sources

Adaskin, Eleanor Jean. 1987. *Stress-Resistance in Relocated Families: Hardiness and Healthy Family Functioning as Mediators of the Stress-Strain Relationship*, Ph.D. Diss., University of Texas, Austin.

Aspinwall, Lisa, and Shelley Taylor. 1997. A Stitch in Time. *Psychological Bulletin* 121:417–443.

Baldwin, Mark W., and John G. Holmes. 1987. Salient Private Audiences and Awareness of the Self. *Journal of Personality and Social Psychology* 52:1087–1098.

Baumeister, Roy F. 1986. *Identity: Cultural Change and the Struggle for Self*. New York and Oxford, Eng.: Oxford University Press.

Belk, Russell W. 1988. Possessions and the Extended Self. *Journal of Consumer Research* 15:139–168.

———. 1992. Moving Possessions: An Analysis Based on Personal Documents from the 1847–1869 Mormon Migration. *Journal of Consumer Research* 19:339–361.

Bridges, William. 1995. *JobShift: How to Prosper in a Workplace Without Jobs*. Reading, Mass.: Addison-Wesley.

Bryan, Mark, Julia Cameron, and Catherine Allen. 1998. *The Artist's Way at Work: Riding the Dragon*. New York: William Morrow.

Cameron, Julia. 1992. *The Artist's Way: A Spiritual Path to Higher Creativity*. New York: G. P. Putnam's Sons.

Caspi, Avshalom. 1993. Why Maladaptive Behaviors Persist: Sources of Continuity and Change Across the Life Course. In *Studying Lives Through Time: Personality and Development*, edited by David C. Funder, Ross D. Parke, Carol Tomlinson-Keasey, and Keith

Widaman. Washington, D.C.: American Psychological Association.

Cialdini, Robert. 1988. *Influence: Science and Practice*. Boston: Scott-Foresman.

Clark, Margaret S. 1984. Record Keeping in Two Types of Relationships. *Journal of Personality and Social Psychology* 47(3):549–557.

Conway, Jill Ker. 1995. *True North: A Memoir*. New York: Vintage Press.

Csikszentmihalyi, Mihaly, and Eugene Rochberg-Halton. 1981. *The Meaning of Things: Domestic Symbols and the Self*. New York: Cambridge University Press.

Feldman, Roberta M. 1990. Settlement, Identity, Psychological Bonds with Home Place in a Mobile Society. *Environment and Behavior* 22:183.

Fischer, Claude S., and C. Ann Stueve. 1977. "Authentic Community:" The Role of Place in Modern Life. In *Networks and Places: Social Relations in the Urban Setting*, edited by Claude S. Fischer. New York: The Free Press.

Fisher, Shirley. 1989. *Homesickness, Cognition and Health*. Hillsdale, N.J.: Lawrence Erlbaum.

Ford, Richard. 1992. An Urge for Going, *Harper's* 284:60.

Gerson, Kathleen, C. Ann Stueve, and Claude S. Fischer. 1977. Attachment to Place. In *Networks and Places: Social Relations in the Urban Setting*, edited by Claude S. Fischer. New York: The Free Press.

Golden, Thomas R. 1998. *Swallowed by a Snake: the Gift of the Masculine Side of Healing*, Kensington, Md.: Golden Healing Publications.

Goodwin, Cathy, and Ronald P. Hill. 1998. Commitment to Physical Fitness: Commercial Influences on Long-Term Healthy Consumer Behaviors. *Social Marketing Quarterly* 4:68-83.

Hempel, Donald J., and Igal Ayal. 1977. Transition Rates and Consumption Systems: A Conceptual Framework for Analyzing Buyer Behavior in Housing Markets. In *Consumer and Industrial Buying Behavior*, edited by Arch G. Woodside, Jagdish N. Sheth, and Peter D. Bennett. New York: North-Holland

Hobfoll, Stevan E., and J. P. Stokes. 1989. The Process and Mechanics of Social Support. In *Handbook of Personal Relationships*, edited by Steven W. Duck. New York: John Wiley.

Kahana, Eve, and Boza Kahana. 1983. Environmental Continuity, Futurity and Adaptation of the Aged. In *Aging and Milieu: Environmental Perspectives on Growing Old*, edited by Graham D. Rowles and Russel J. Ohta. New York: Academic Press.

Kamerman, Jack B. 1986. *Death in the Midst of Life: Social and Cultural Influences on Death, Grief and Mourning.* Englewood Cliffs, N.J.: Prentice-Hall.

Korosec-Serafty, Perla. 1984. The Home, from Attic to Cellar. *Journal of Environmental Psychology* 4:172–179.

Lieberman, Morton. 1992. Perceptions of Changes in the Self: The Impact of Life Events and Large Group Awareness Training. In *Self Change: Social Psychological and Clinical Perspectives.* New York: Springer-Verlag.

———. 1996. *Doors Close, Doors Open: Widows, Grieving and Growing.* New York: Putnam.

Mandler, George. 1990. Interruption Theory in *On the Move: The Psychology of Change and Transition,* edited by Shirley Fisher and C. L. Cooper. New York: John Wiley and Sons.

Marcus, Clare Cooper. 1995. *House as a Mirror of Self: Exploring the Deeper Meaning of Home.* Berkeley, Calif.: Conari Press.

Martin, Linda Carroll. 1998. The Apple is Shinier, but I Miss the Worms. *New York Times,* Money and Business section, February 22.

McCollum, Audrey T. 1990. *The Trauma of Moving: Psychological Issues for Women.* Newbury Park, Calif.: Sage Publications.

McKay, Matthew, and Patrick Fanning. 1992. *Self-Esteem.* Oakland, Calif.: New Harbinger Publications.

McKay, Matthew, Patrick Fanning, and Martha Davis. 1997. *Thoughts and Feelings: Taking Control of Your Moods and Your Life.* Oakland, Calif.: New Harbinger Publications.

Milgram, Stanley. 1977. *The Individual in a Social World.* Reading, Mass.: Addison-Wesley.

Montanino, Fred. 1984. Protecting the Federal Witness: Burying Past Life in Biography. *American Behavioral Scientist* 27:501–528.

Munton, Anthony G. 1990. Job Relocation, Stress and the Family. *Journal of Organizational Behavior* 11:401–406.

———. 1993. *Job Relocation: Managing People on the Move.* New York: John Wiley Publications.

Myss, Caroline. 1997. *Why People Don't Heal and How They Can.* New York: Three Rivers Press.

Pescosolido, Bernice A. 1986. Migration, Medical Care Preferences and the Lay Referral System: A Network Theory of Role Assimilation. *American Sociological Review* 51:523–540.

Prend, Ashley Davis. 1997. *Transcending Loss: Understanding the Lifelong Impact of Grief and How to Make It Meaningful.* Berkeley, Calif.: Berkeley Publishing Group.

Raviv, Amiram, Giora Keinan, Yehuda Abazon, and Alona Raviv. 1990. Moving as a Stressful Life Event for Adolescents. *Journal of Community Psychology* 18 (April) 130–140.

Riesman, David, and Harold Roseborough. 1955. Careers in Consumer Behavior. In *Consumer Behavior II: The Life Cycle and Consumer Behavior*, edited by L. Clark. New York: New York University Press.

Silverman, David. 1993. *Interpreting Qualitative Data: Methods for Analysing Talk, Text and Interaction*. Beverly Hills, Calif.: Sage Publications.

Sluzki, Carlos E. 1986. Migration and Family Conflict. In *Coping with Life Crises: An Integrated Approach*, edited by Rudolf H. Moos. New York: Plenum Press.

Storr, Anthony. 1988. *Solitude: A Return to the Self*. New York: Ballentine Books.

Tait, Rosemary, and Roxane Cohen Silver. 1989. Coming to Terms with Major Negative Life Events. In *Unintended Thought*, edited by James S. Uleman and John A. Bargh. New York and London: Guilford Press.

Tannen, Deborah. 1986. *That's Not What I Meant!: How Conversational Style Makes or Breaks Your Relations with Others*. New York: Morrow.

Tatelbaum, Judy. 1980. *The Courage to Grieve*. New York: Harper's.

United States Bureau of the Census 1990. Current Population Reports. In *Statistical Abstract of the United States*. 19.

Von Zeller, Hubert. 1951. *We Sing While There's Voice Left*. London and New York: Sheed and Ward.

Weiss, Robert S. 1990. Losses Associated with Mobility. In *On the Move: The Psychology of Change and Transition*, edited by Shirley Fisher and C. L. Cooper. New York: John Wiley & Sons.

Zimbardo, Philip. 1991. The Joys of Being a Psychologist. Presentation at American Psychological Association, San Francisco. Recorded on tape APA 91–200.

More New Harbinger Titles

SIX KEYS TO CREATING THE LIFE YOU DESIRE

Helps you learn how to build a sense of trust, acknowledge your accomplishments, stop comparing yourself to others, achieve closeness, stop doubting your competence, and identify a core purpose that will let you follow through on your dreams.   *Item KEY6 $19.95*

HIGH ON STRESS

A variety of enlightening exercises help women rethink the role of stress in their lives, rework their physical and mental responses to it, and find ways to boost the potentially positive impact that stress can have on their well-being.
Item HOS $13.95

WORKING ANGER

A step-by-step program designed to help anyone who has had trouble dealing with their own anger or other people's anger at work.
Item WA Paperback $12.95

WANTING WHAT YOU HAVE: A Self-Discovery Workbook

This step-by-step workbook shows you how proven cognitive therapy principles can help make it possible to achieve contentment and meet the challenges of modern life with balance and serenity.   *Item WANT Paperback, $18.95*

SEX SMART

"Sex Smart is the book on everything you probably didn't know about why you turned out the way you did sexually—and what to do about it."
—Arnold Lazarus, Ph.D.   *Item SESM $14.95*

CLAIMING YOUR CREATIVE SELF

The inspiring stories of thirteen women who were able to keep in touch with their own creative spirit opens the door to new definitions of creativity, and to the kinds of transforming ideas that will change your life.   *Item CYCS $15.95*

Call **toll-free 1-800-748-6273** to order. Have your Visa or Mastercard number ready. Or send a check for the titles you want to New Harbinger Publications, 5674 Shattuck Avenue, Oakland, CA 94609. Include $3.80 for the first book and 75¢ for each additional book to cover shipping and handling. (California residents please include appropriate sales tax.) Allow four to six weeks for delivery.

Prices subject to change without notice.

Some Other New Harbinger Self-Help Titles

Claiming Your Creative Self: True Stories from the Everyday Lives of Women, $15.95
Six Keys to Creating the Life You Desire, $19.95
Taking Control of TMJ, $13.95
What You Need to Know About Alzheimer's, $15.95
Winning Against Relapse: A Workbook of Action Plans for Recurring Health and Emotional Problems, $14.95
Facing 30: Women Talk About Constructing a Real Life and Other Scary Rites of Passage, $12.95
The Worry Control Workbook, $15.95
Wanting What You Have: A Self-Discovery Workbook, $18.95
When Perfect Isn't Good Enough: Strategies for Coping with Perfectionism, $13.95
The Endometriosis Survival Guide, $13.95
Earning Your Own Respect: A Handbook of Personal Responsibility, $12.95
High on Stress: A Woman's Guide to Optimizing the Stress in Her Life, $13.95
Infidelity: A Survival Guide, $13.95
Stop Walking on Eggshells, $14.95
Consumer's Guide to Psychiatric Drugs, $16.95
The Fibromyalgia Advocate: Getting the Support You Need to Cope with Fibromyalgia and Myofascial Pain, $18.95
Healing Fear: New Approaches to Overcoming Anxiety, $16.95
Working Anger: Preventing and Resolving Conflict on the Job, $12.95
Sex Smart: How Your Childhood Shaped Your Sexual Life and What to Do About It, $14.95
You Can Free Yourself From Alcohol & Drugs, $13.95
Amongst Ourselves: A Self-Help Guide to Living with Dissociative Identity Disorder, $14.95
Healthy Living with Diabetes, $13.95
Dr. Carl Robinson's Basic Baby Care, $10.95
Better Boundaries: Owning and Treasuring Your Life, $13.95
Goodbye Good Girl, $12.95
Being, Belonging, Doing, $10.95
Thoughts & Feelings, Second Edition, $18.95
Depression: How It Happens, How It's Healed, $14.95
Trust After Trauma, $15.95
The Chemotherapy & Radiation Survival Guide, Second Edition, $14.95
Surviving Childhood Cancer, $12.95
The Headache & Neck Pain Workbook, $14.95
Perimenopause, $16.95
The Self-Forgiveness Handbook, $12.95
A Woman's Guide to Overcoming Sexual Fear and Pain, $14.95
Don't Take It Personally, $12.95
Becoming a Wise Parent For Your Grown Child, $12.95
Clear Your Past, Change Your Future, $13.95
Preparing for Surgery, $17.95
The Power of Two, $15.95
It's Not OK Anymore, $13.95
The Daily Relaxer, $12.95
The Body Image Workbook, $17.95
Living with ADD, $17.95
When Anger Hurts Your Kids, $12.95
The Chronic Pain Control Workbook, Second Edition, $17.95
Fibromyalgia & Chronic Myofascial Pain Syndrome, $19.95
Kid Cooperation: How to Stop Yelling, Nagging & Pleading and Get Kids to Cooperate, $13.95
The Stop Smoking Workbook: Your Guide to Healthy Quitting, $17.95
Conquering Carpal Tunnel Syndrome and Other Repetitive Strain Injuries, $17.95
An End to Panic: Breakthrough Techniques for Overcoming Panic Disorder, Second Edition, $18.95
Letting Go of Anger: The 10 Most Common Anger Styles and What to Do About Them, $12.95
Messages: The Communication Skills Workbook, Second Edition, $15.95
Coping With Chronic Fatigue Syndrome: Nine Things You Can Do, $13.95
The Anxiety & Phobia Workbook, Second Edition, $18.95
The Relaxation & Stress Reduction Workbook, Fourth Edition, $17.95
Living Without Depression & Manic Depression: A Workbook for Maintaining Mood Stability, $18.95
Coping With Schizophrenia: A Guide For Families, $15.95
Visualization for Change, Second Edition, $15.95
Angry All the Time: An Emergency Guide to Anger Control, $12.95
Couple Skills: Making Your Relationship Work, $14.95
Self-Esteem, Second Edition, $13.95
I Can't Get Over It, A Handbook for Trauma Survivors, Second Edition, $16.95
Dying of Embarrassment: Help for Social Anxiety and Social Phobia, $13.95
The Depression Workbook: Living With Depression and Manic Depression, $17.95
Men & Grief: A Guide for Men Surviving the Death of a Loved One, $14.95
When Once Is Not Enough: Help for Obsessive Compulsives, $14.95
Beyond Grief: A Guide for Recovering from the Death of a Loved One, $14.95
Hypnosis for Change: A Manual of Proven Techniques, Third Edition, $15.95
When Anger Hurts, $13.95